Ua

STOP
BULLYING ME

MARIE-CLAIRE RUPIO

BALBOA.PRESS
A DIVISION OF HAY HOUSE

Balboa Press books may be ordered through booksellers or by contacting:

Balboa Press
A Division of Hay House
1663 Liberty Drive
Bloomington, IN 47403
www.balboapress.co.uk
UK TFN: 0800 0148647 (Toll Free inside the UK)
UK Local: 02036 956325 (+44 20 3695 6325 from outside the UK)

Because of the dynamic nature of the Internet, any web addresses or
links contained in this book may have changed since publication and
may no longer be valid. The views expressed in this work are solely those
of the author and do not necessarily reflect the views of the publisher,
and the publisher hereby disclaims any responsibility for them.

The author of this book does not dispense medical advice or prescribe the use
of any technique as a form of treatment for physical, emotional, or medical
problems without the advice of a physician, either directly or indirectly. The
intent of the author is only to offer information of a general nature to help
you in your quest for emotional and spiritual well-being. In the event you use
any of the information in this book for yourself, which is your constitutional
right, the author and the publisher assume no responsibility for your actions.

Any people depicted in stock imagery provided by Getty Images are
models, and such images are being used for illustrative purposes only.
Certain stock imagery © Getty Images.

Print information available on the last page.

ISBN: 978-1-9822-8219-6 (sc)
ISBN: 978-1-9822-8288-2 (e)

Balboa Press rev. date: 01/07/2021

PREVIEW

The book starts out by talking about a hard but lovely childhood that led to some poor choices and hurtful treatment throughout a young girl's life. These negative situations continued until she was older, and they never really stopped.

After dealing with a tremendous amount of bullying, she was broken and wounded. Knowing that she had only herself and her parents to rely on, she later found the courage to move out of this situation and find her own path.

This is the journey of Delilah's life throughout a period of bullying, self-distraction and low self-esteem.

In this book, Delilah goes through the darkest, saddest, and happiest moments of her life. She tries to see the light at the end of the tunnel and still has faith. She goes through humiliations, hurtful words, and painful acceptance. She finds it hard to accept herself the way she is, because everybody seems to want her to be different, pulling her in every direction. She believes she will get through it, but she doesn't know how long she can hold it together. She tries to be happy and independent, but it doesn't always happen the way she wants.

In the end, she hopes everything will come together in the right direction, and she prays that God knows what is coming.

But can she manage her life after the breakdown?

Will she ever be able to fully trust again?

This book invites us to focus on our own paths and not on others'.

AUTHOR'S NOTE

Welcome and thank you for reading my book. My name is Marie-Claire. I am 25 years old, and this is my first book.

I live with my fiancé and our three lovely kids in a small village in the United Kingdom. We were in lockdown for a few months here in the UK, so my mother and I talked about my life and my future. Because we didn't have a lot to do during lockdown except entertain our kids, I started writing my own book.

It didn't come as easily as I hoped it would, but I am very proud that I was able to write it down and share it with the world.

I never was into writing before. In school, I never really showed much interest. My passion was to dance my whole life, even now. But when I got pregnant, a lot of things changed. I am very proud and happy about how I have turned out, and I am excited about what more is coming in my life.

I had education as a make-up artist five years ago as well, and I am still working in that industry. Writing is a totally new chapter in my life, but I am very excited to see how my life will change with this new open door.

I do hope that this book will help others see that they

are not alone in any situation and that they can overcome challenges in life.

I do hope that you will enjoy my book and maybe recommend it to someone you know who goes through a similar situation. Happy reading, and stay blessed.

MARKETING HEADLINE

We are living in a world where so many problems don't get the attention they deserve. Bullying, cyberbullying, racism, and much more are underestimated in every part of the world. People say it will be OK one day, but how can they be sure, if no one is learning how to actually do something about it? Most people are simply watching and observing, too scared to do anything.

I invite you to read this book if you want to see a change in this world in at least one subject that has been highly active the past few years. Take a step towards the people who need help and who are not able to help themselves. Let them know they are not alone, because as we know, we are all one race, the human race. We are all in this together, and God knows why.

DELILAH SUMMARY

Delilah is a wonderful, loving, brave, and beautiful girl. She is a small girl with long blonde hair and lovely curls. Her passion is dancing and singing every day. Her way of life involves believing things will have a positive ending; even when one walks through storms, better days will come. Her dream is to be the light in a dark world. Some people who know her would say she is too nice to other people, even to the ones who don't deserve it. She lives in a small village with her two parents and her older brother. Her grandmother and grandfather live next to them. She is very spiritual, believes in God, and thinks good about everybody.

Most of the time, even when others can't see it, she is very vulnerable and cares about the needs of others more than her own. She has a big, bright light in her soul that some people are scared of because she shines so brightly, it frightens them.

She believes that everyone is good inside and out. But she also knows that a lot of people have a dark side within them.

Her heart is clean and pure, and she wants to live every day and enjoy her life with everything she has.

God is a big part of her life, and you will see throughout this book that God is always by her side in good and bad times.

CHAPTER 1

CHILD

I was 4 years old when I went to a nursery the first time, with my baby friend Emily. Our parents had known each other for a very long time. Emily and I did everything together because we didn't live far apart from each other, about a five-minute walk. We went two days a week to the nursery. I didn't like it at all. Every day my mum left me at the nursery, I started crying. I always had my little donkey with me, who would protect and calm me down when I felt sad.

As we started the nursery, Emily made friends with a boy called Leo. I was friends with him too, but I wasn't really keen on him because he was not nice to me a lot of times.

The next day, I brought my little donkey, and the second I arrived, Leo took the little donkey from me and threw it away. Little did I know that Emily would support him. Emily and Leo shouted at me, "You are too old to have a donkey. You are not a baby." Yes, my best friend Emily supported him.

After a while, a teacher came over and saw me crying. "Why are you crying?" she asked. I pointed my finger towards my friends and started to cry again. The teacher took the baby donkey from them and told them to apologize. They did, but with a big smile.

Surprisingly, after a while we got along really well with Leo, but I was never really delighted to play with him.

As a young child, I tried to forget and pretend it didn't happen because I wanted to play with my best friend. I just wanted to be happy.

When we got a bit older, we also had birthday parties together, and we really enjoyed them. Everybody did at that age, I guess. We had pool parties at Emily's house and barbecue with our families as well.

The time came when I turned seven and had to start primary school. Emily and I went to the same school and were in the same class, of course. We even sat next to each other.

Just as school started, I got sick. I had some seizures with a high temperature. The doctors explained that the seizures came because of the high temperature, so they didn't do any further tests that time. My mum wanted them to do more tests because after every vaccination, I had a high temperature and seizures. One time I received a vaccination and immediately had a seizure without any temperature.

My parents took me to the hospital to get me checked up. My parents were sure that there was something wrong with me. The doctors looked at me and could see something wasn't right. I was very pale, and my teeth had some white spots. In that moment, they decided that I had to stay with my mum in the hospital for two weeks. I was out of school and with no friends.

It took two weeks until they figured out what I had.

They did a lot of exams on my brain, as well as blood tests. After two weeks, the doctors came and said, "We know what she has." My mum was happy that finally they had found out the reason behind all this. They said, "It's hyperparathyroidism". There are problems with her epithelial bodies next to the thyroid. They stopped working, so she can't take calcium on her own."

My mum looked at the doctor and asked, "So what do we have to do, and how is that possible?" She was confused.

The doctor explained what I had to take every day and added that I shouldn't miss it. When the calcium went down again, I could suffer another seizure—or something worse. They gave me the medicine to take and sent me home.

I hated it because it had a really bad smell while I drank it. I was still a child, so I thought that I didn't really need it. I didn't want to take my illness seriously at that time. I thought that maybe it would go away again. When we went home and I went back to school, sometimes I hid the liquid (that was in a package) behind the couch or anywhere my parents wouldn't see them. Yes, it was a really bad idea.

Unfortunately, one day my parents had to move and clean behind the couch, and they saw some pills on the ground. My parents were very angry with me and told me that I shouldn't do this because the pills were important for my health. I tried to understand because I saw the fear in my parents' eyes. I tried to explain that I couldn't stand the smell of the medicine. My mum looked at me and said, "You can't do this again. You are risking your health." I apologized and gave her a big hug.

After a week, my mum talked to my doctor and got me some new pills that I could swallow. I didn't love it, but it was fine with me. I simply wanted my parents to be happy. "Anything is better than drinking it now I can just take it with a sip of water. And not the liquid with that awful smell," I said.

When I was back in school, I was really quiet. I liked my teachers and friends but was really shy and didn't like to say anything out loud. I missed a lot in school, so for the first weeks, I felt a bit left out, even though my friends supported me and tried to teach me everything they learned.

I liked my main teacher but didn't know that he told my mum I was too quiet in class and claimed it was my mum's fault. How could a teacher say a child was too quiet in class just because I didn't scream like all the others? I respected them, so I did not shout to say the answer. My mum was really angry about it but didn't tell me anything because she didn't want to ruin my view of him as the nice teacher. School was never easy for me. I usually knew the answers but was too shy to act loud like all the other children, shouting and screaming. I enjoyed some classes, except sports and maths.

What I did love after school was ballet. I started early and made friends quickly with a girl named Lucy. Lucy and I were good friends, and we met up to have play dates quite often. We always went to ballet together.

We had our first big performance, and my ballet teacher chose me and Lucy to be the main character, but just one of us could go on the main day Madame Blaire chose me to go ahead and be the first main character to dance. It was my first big performance. I was so proud of myself when she mentioned my name. As one would expect, Lucy wasn't pleased with it, but she had to take it because Madame Blaire had decided.

The day came, and everybody was there—my parents, my grandmother, some friends of my parents, and of course my brother. I was really nervous and tried to smile when I had to go out and perform, but I looked down. I wanted to do everything right in front of everyone, so I forgot to look up and smile. I trained so hard for this to be perfect. In that moment, I did all the right steps perfectly, but with no smile. As everybody clapped for me, I was happy, and everyone could see a small smile on my face.

After all the shows, my grandmother checked the newspaper and saw a photo of me at my performance. It was just me in the newspaper because I was the first main character to perform. There was no Lucy.

My mum was really keen with her mum, so they talked often; her family also knew about my illness.

After a while, a big company for ballet reached out to our teacher and wanted me to come. They had seen the show and liked the way I danced. Lucy and her mum didn't like it, so when they heard about it, they went to the teacher and said that I wouldn't be able to do it because of my illness. Because of that, the teacher said that the ballet company changed their minds and didn't want me to come anymore. I believed what the teacher said, but my mum always thought that it wasn't because of that reason. My mum told me that she talked to Lucy's mum about it, and Lucy's mum acted oddly. We would never find out what exactly was said.

As a child, I tried to move on and forget as quickly as possible because I didn't believe people could be so mean and would make decisions for someone else behind one's back.

After that, Lucy and I played well together like nothing had happened. Sometimes I thought about the way Lucy was towards me and why Lucy was pushing me away, but if I went too far from her, she would come back right away. Lucy was always the first to speak up about what we would play that day. If she wasn't good at what we were doing, we would stop. Lucy always turned the tables: instead of saying she wasn't good at it, she said I was the worst. Lucy would never admit she wasn't good at something.

I loved Lucy's house very much. It was quite big and dreamy, and that was why I didn't mind her mean words sometimes. I enjoyed playing there and being friends with Lucy. I always dreamed of having a good friendship, and I saw the good in everyone because I didn't believe there were bad people in the world, especially when they told me they were my friends.

One day after ballet class, I went to Lucy's house. Her grandmother had a big pool and a sauna next to it. We were so happy when her grandmother allowed us to go in. That day it was very warm. We went for a swim inside the pool straight away.

After some time, Lucy wanted to go to the sauna for fun, but it turned in another direction. I was scared of the sauna because it was really hot inside, and it was a very small room. I asked Lucy not to close the door when she went out because I would feel scared.

Lucy went out, closed the door behind her, and locked it. She laughed about it for a long time. I told her to open the door and immediately started to panic and cry. Lucy laughed and didn't even care. She said that she couldn't find the key, but she didn't even made an effort to find it.

Finally, after some minutes, her grandmother came and opened it up. She was angry with Lucy but not as angry as she should have been. After that, I wanted to go home, and thankfully my mum came at the right time. I was so relieved that my mum was there and I was able to go home. Lucy smiled and said, "I had a good time. See you tomorrow." I glared at her and went to the car.

That evening, I went to my room to hear some music, and I tried to not think about it again. I didn't tell my parents about it and kept it to myself.

Everybody had summer break, so Lucy, my parents, and I went to Spain to enjoy some sun. I was very happy that I was allowed to bring a friend along.

We had a very nice hotel, good food, and a lot of entertainment during the day and night. Lucy and I loved to swim in the big pool and stayed inside the whole day. One day when we went for dinner, Lucy asked my dad if he liked her more than his own daughter. My dad looked at her very confused and said, "She is my daughter." He shook his head and was quite angry. I looked at Lucy and wondered how she could even ask my dad that question. How did she think he would answer?

We didn't talk about it again, and I tried to forget and enjoy our holiday together.

Some evenings, we saw dance shows. Lucy and I were so overwhelmed with the dance. We loved it and couldn't take our eyes from the show. After two weeks of sun and ocean, we sadly had to go back home for our last year in primary school.

Primary school was almost finished, but one girl, named Nicola, came to my class and had to repeat the last year. She was very friendly but kind of shy. She sat next to me because one seat was free at my table. We talked and played together during the breaks. Emily and Nicola didn't really liked each other much. And Emily often got jealous because I played with Nicola more than with her.

One day after school, Nicola invited me to have some lunch with her family. It was so nice of her to ask, and of course I went. We discovered that we had so much in common, we liked the same music, loved dancing, and made funny videos. The best part was we had a lot of imagination. Sometimes we filmed a music video and acted like Lady Gaga or Christina Aguilera. It was funny, and we enjoyed it so much. Every time I came over to her house or she came to my place, we did a new video. The time with her made me feel very happy.

I was lucky to have had a friend like Nicola by my side. She was as crazy as I was.

I was a very spiritual girl like my mother, but I didn't always say what I could see. I always saw the good in people and not the shadows they were hiding. One day when my parents were working late—they were musicians and had to perform late on the weekends—I slept at my grandmother's house. I liked it because I was allowed to eat everything and stay up late. During the evening, when we were all watching TV, I looked outside and saw a bright light walking past the window. I stared at the window for a while and saw what I thought were some wings. First I was scared, but then I looked closer, and that bright light sent a warm energy to me. Immediately I told my grandfather. Soon after, he went outside and looked around the house but couldn't see anything or anybody.

The next morning, my parents picked me up and took me home. I told my mum about the bright light walking past the window. She smiled at me and said, "Good you have seen it. I sent it to you so you would be protected."

Even when people don't believe in God or other things, they do exist. These people simply don't allow spirits or angels to come near them, so they can't see them. Be open for it, because it is real.

Let's get back to my friendship with Nicola. One vacation, I invited Nicola to come with me and my parents to Portugal, to enjoy a holiday together. Nicola was so happy that I invited her to come, and she said yes.

When the time came, we packed our things and went to the Algarve. It was a four-hour flight, but it didn't matter when we reached the hotel. The weather was hot, and even in the evening it was still warm.

We had a nice hotel room with three beds. Nicola and I slept in the one in front of the balcony. We loved the view upon waking up every morning. The first day we went out to the pool, settled in some chairs, and lay down with my parents. Both of us were looking around and enjoying the sun. After some time, we wanted to go to the beach, which was just down the stairs.

We took some towels and one sun umbrella. The sun was really strong, and we got red real quick. We searched a place to put our towels and umbrella down, and then we went into the ocean. There were big waves, and over time we tried to go inside the water, but in that second a big wave hit us, and we were underwater. We laughed and enjoyed it, even when our hair was all over our faces.

After some time in the water, we lay down under our sun umbrella. Nicola said, "Wait, why is it so light under the umbrella?" We opened our eyes and saw that our umbrella had just flown away. We jumped up and ran after the umbrella. I bet it was pretty funny for everybody to see. When we finally caught the umbrella, we couldn't breathe because we laughed so hard the entire way back to our spot. Some people who lay next to us smiled at us. Nicola and I could read their minds, because that was funny.

After that small adventure on the beach, we went upstairs to the room and met my parents for dinner. We all took a quick shower and dressed nice, like every evening. When we waited for our seats, we looked down the hill and smiled. We were happy, and everybody could see that.

After a week, sadly we had to go home. We didn't want to it because was much better here than at home. When we reached the airport, we waved goodbye to the ocean and went inside the airplane. When we reached home, Nicola's parents were already waiting at the airport. They hugged and smiled at everybody. Nicola looked at me and said, "I hope we will do this again. I loved it," and she hugged me tight.

When I reached home, I fell into my bed and slept straight away. It was a long and tiring trip, and everybody was tired.

CHAPTER 2

PAIN

After we finished primary school, we had to decide to which school to go. My grades weren't too good, so the school recommended that I go to the second school. People who went there were good at school but needed a bit more support. Then there was the first high school, where all the smart asses went. Emily and her mum decided to let her go to the first school, so my mum and I decided to give it a try as well. Emily and I were still together every day.

As a surprise, we found out that Lucy would also come to the school with us, and eventually we all came into the same class. We were very happy, or at least I was, because I was able to be with Emily and Lucy at the same time. Emily didn't really liked Lucy, so she wasn't too happy about it. But at that time I didn't really care about her opinion. Emily always said that there was something odd about Lucy she didn't like. I didn't really see, or I didn't want to see it.

On our first day of school, we were so happy and excited that we jumped up and down, full of joy to finally be in the big girls' school. The school was huge, and the people were nice. We were able to choose our seats for the first month, so I chose to sit next to Emily and Lucy.

After a while, I made friends with a girl named Veronica, and I immediately liked her. She seemed confident, funny, and smart. We got along well. She helped me during class, was always by my side, and supported me in everything. I talked to her about everything that was going on in my life. She knew everything about me, and I knew a lot about her. Because of her, I got through the first months of school.

I loved spending time with Veronica more than with Emily. She made me feel loved and confident. Her mother was friendly too and saw me as a part of her family. Everybody in her family was open to everyone and welcomed me with open arms. We had a lot of sleepovers and play dates, and we did everything together. Veronica and I spent every second together. It was like nothing could get between us.

When we had our next vacation for two weeks, Veronica invited me to come camping with her family. I immediately said yes and was so happy when my parents allowed me to go with them. The day came where I packed all my stuff, and we started our journey. It was a very long drive, but the minute we arrived,

Veronica and I went straight to the beach and enjoyed the sun. I got a sunburn all over my body, as did Veronica. But no one cared about it; we simply smiled it out and moved on. Every day we played in the sun. We even tried some volleyball. The first attempts didn't go so well, but at least we gave it a try.

On that vacation, we both had a lot of things to do. We went for a swim late at night and enjoyed time together. One day we were riding our bicycle downhill, and suddenly Veronica had her steering wheel in her hands. We both looked shocked, but right after we laughed. After a minute passed, Veronica tried to stop and went straight into the bushes. She laughed so hard that she couldn't breathe. We both laughed the whole way back home and tried to fix her bike. It got fixed, but we clearly never did it again.

After two weeks, we sadly had to go back home because the school was about to start again. The day we came home, I felt even closer to Veronica, like we had some deep connection, a special friendship.

After school started again, Lucy started to like Veronica as well. They both got close but never left me out of the group. One afternoon, Lucy and I had a our ballet class. It was very different than usual. Lucy clearly acted strange towards me. She talked to one girl, named Anita, about me and laughed. I heard them saying my name several times.

Anita was a friend of mine as well and was always nice to me, at least when no one else was around. We all had the same ballet class. I loved dancing; it had been my passion since my first class. I knew I wanted to be a dancer one day and show my skills to everyone. But in that class, I thought that I wouldn't make it because everybody said that I should be more like Lucy, simply because she was faker than me. She seemed to be more confident in doing things and had a big, fake smile on her face. I knew a good smile was necessary for a good dancer because one needed to make a show and entertain the people. But the smile Lucy did wasn't about passion or about dance; it was forced. In that moment, no one cared. As such, I thought I would never have a chance in the industry, but I never gave up. I kept practicing it and tried to focus on myself. I tried to not get distracted by anyone. I followed my dream.

One day we had our French class. Lucy sat in the back

of the class, and I sat in front with Veronica. That day everything changed. When I came into the class and went to my seat, Lucy sat next to Veronica, smiled at her, and said, "Today I am sitting here. You can sit in my seat."

I looked at her confused but couldn't say anything. I then looked at Veronica, but she just looked away. I took a deep breath and went to the back of the class. Of course I wasn't happy about it, but what else could I do or say? I didn't want to make Lucy upset, and I didn't want to make a big scene out of it, so I did as Lucy said. My feelings were all over the place, and I wasn't sure how to feel about it. I heard Veronica and Lucy laughing and looking at me that day. I had a weird feeling about it because Veronica didn't say anything or show any sign to Lucy that I should have been allowed to sit there. In that moment, I wanted to scream and shout at Lucy for sitting in my seat. But I couldn't; I was too kind to do so, so I kept quiet.

During the class, our French teacher wanted us to move the tables so we could work in a circle. I moved one table and tried to push it over. "Let me help you," Lucy said. She held the table at the other end of it but pushed it the wrong way. Suddenly I felt a lot of pain in my fingers. My fingers were stuck between two tables. "Oh, I am so sorry. I didn't see the other table." She laughed. I looked at her, slightly smiled, and said, "It's fine."

After that incident, I couldn't say or do anything because I was shocked. I wanted to go up to Lucy and tell her that she sucked. But no, I would never be mean to a person who was my friend.

At the end, our French teacher wanted to talk to me after that class, so I stayed a bit longer and listened to her.

My teacher said that I should be very careful with Lucy and Veronica. I didn't fit in with them, and she knew that I wasn't like them. I was the light in every room, but right now my light was dragged down and pushed aside because of them. They didn't let me shine.

I looked at her and said, "You don't need to worry. They are my friends." The teacher replied, "Just think about how real friends should treat you." That time my teacher made me think about all she said. But even though Lucy was mean to me, I didn't really see it as a threat. She was my friend, and I couldn't believe that she meant it in a bad way.

I was so happy when that class was over, and I went to the next class and sat next to Veronica again because our English teacher didn't want any changes in the seating plan. Veronica talked to me as normal as possible like nothing was wrong, and we didn't talk about French class. Veronica looked at me and said, "You are a good friend." I was so happy and said it back. But right after, she smiled and turned to Lucy.

When school finished, I was supposed to go to Veronica's house, just her and me, but suddenly she said, "Lucy wants to come as well, and she will sleep at my house, so you need someone to pick you up." I looked at her and just said OK, but I felt sad and confused.

The day wasn't as usual. When we went to Veronica's house, her mother focused on Lucy, not me. It was like I wasn't even there. I hated it because when we were with Lucy, it was not as usual. Lucy and Veronica never waited for me when we walked outside. They simply ran away and hid behind a bush or a car, and I had to find them. Sometimes I had to walk home alone because Veronica and

Lucy ran home before me. I wanted to go home every time, but I wouldn't say because I thought that would make a big problem from it when there was none. Veronica and I always had so much fun together. We played a game on the computer or danced. But with the three of us, there was nothing fun for me.

After that meeting, we always had to meet up as the three of us. Veronica and Lucy were glued together, and no one could separate them. I couldn't stand it because every time I became close to someone, Lucy would steal that person away. Sometimes I got lucky to be with just Veronica, and it felt good because we had so much in common. It was like we were sisters again, and no one disturbed our connection.

After some time, Lucy, Veronica, and I seemed to get along pretty well. At least, it seemed that way to me. We talked to each other about everything and were good in school.

Emily came to me one day and asked me about a meet-up. Of course I said yes. After school, I went to her place. Emily looked at me and said, "You know I don't like Veronica or Lucy, because I have a feeling there is something going on, and I don't want you to get hurt." I told her she shouldn't worry about it because everything was fine, but I appreciated the concern.

After a few months, Emily told me that she had to change to a lower school because her grades weren't getting any better; she did struggle to keep up with the classes. I was surprised because I didn't really know; I wasn't with her as much as before.

The lower school where she would go was next to my

school, so it was possible for us to still see each other during breaks. She told me that she was much happier at that school. Every morning, Emily and I went together to school and talked a lot, but after some time it stopped. I thought that she had found good friends and so didn't have any time for me again, but that time it didn't bother me too much because I had Veronica.

A new girl came to our class, and her name was Caro. She had recently moved from Munich. She was a shy but friendly girl, and her way of smiling was so warm that it made others smile.

Lucy, Veronica, and I approached her, but one could see that she wasn't really keen with Veronica or Lucy. She did like me, so she tried to talk to me. We discovered that we liked the same music, so we had some things to talk about. She showed me that I could trust her and talk to her.

After some time, Caro and I met up, and she asked me about a singing contest at our school. She loved singing as much as I did, so of course I said yes. When we started to sing songs together for our big performance, we got even closer.

Lucy and Veronica always tried to come along with Caro, but it was not possible because she wasn't really interest in a friendship with them. Every day one could see that they were very jealous about the fact that I was able to get along with her and they couldn't.

Veronica and I still met up as usual, and sometimes with Lucy too. With Lucy, I went once a week to our ballet classes. We still danced together and drove to our classes together. But honestly, I was very happy that I didn't need to do anything more with Lucy.

The big day came of our big performance for the singing contest in school. Caro and I were ready to show our songs and dance. Veronica and Lucy were in the first row to show their support. We sang, danced, and had a lot of fun performing. After the song was done, everybody clapped and cheered. Unfortunately we didn't win, but it was a great experience. After the show, Caro and I hugged tightly and were so happy about what we had done. I knew this friendship was good.

Later that week, something changed. Veronica, Lucy, and Caro acted strange towards me. I saw them together and asked myself how this was possible. Caro didn't like them at all. They stood together in the school hall talking, and the second they saw me, they immediately stopped and said to one of our classmates, "Oh, why don't you get some food for us and take Delilah with you?" The girl agreed.

I looked at them and saw them smiling, so I went with the girl upstairs, and they immediately started talking again. Every time I came near them, they stopped and sent me away again, like it was a joke to them. I did it because I did everything they told me to do, and I didn't think it was anything bad, but I did have a strange feeling inside my body that it was about me. I asked myself why on earth they would even stand together when they never liked each other.

When they finished and I approached them, all three of them smiled at me and were speaking normally. At that time, I thought maybe they were planning something nice for me.

Time passed, and we were already over one year in that school. One day I felt sick during school and wanted to go the sick room, where one could have some rest. I went there by myself because Veronica and Lucy didn't want to go with me. The second I went into the room, I felt even sicker.

I saw my name all over the room. They wrote things like, "Delilah is a bitch. She is ugly, she is fat. What a loser. I hope she dies."

When I read all that I cried ; I didn't understand why people would write this about me. I didn't do anything to anyone, and I always tried to be nice to everyone. My whole world broke down—my friendships and everything that I thought was good for me. My thoughts couldn't stop thinking as I looked at this stupid wall in this room.

That day when I came home, I went straight to my room and went to bed. I was hurt and in so much pain. I tried to understand what was going on. Veronica came to visit me that day alone and asked me what was wrong. I told her about the wall in the sick room. She said, "I have seen it too. It's terrible that people would write this about someone."

I cried, and Veronica gave me a big hug. I tried to forget everything, but two days after that, I went to the sick room again because I had fallen down and scratched my leg. I looked at the wall again, and even more things appeared: "I hope she will kill herself so we have more peace. Too ugly for this world. Who would love her?"

Veronica came into the room and tried to clean up the wall. I was happy that she was there with me.

After a while, I thought about talking to my parents about it, but I didn't want to worry them because I was sure that I had Veronica, and she would never turn me down. She would always be there with me and support me in bad moments. I still put a smile on my face every day and tried to not think about the room.

I tried hard to not think about it, but every time someone said something bad about another person, I immediately started to think about the wall. After some time, the thoughts went away slowly, but they were never really gone.

After a few months, I went to the sick room again out of curiosity. I wanted to see whether the sentences were still on the wall. They were, and by that time I looked at them very closely. I was shocked when I studied the handwriting. It was Veronica's and Lucy's handwriting. I remembered they went often in the sick room a few months back. Of course I didn't want to believe it because they were my friends and wouldn't do such things . . . right? No one would hurt her best friends.

That was what I thought to myself. That was why I didn't speak to them about it, because I didn't want to believe that it could be them. Surprisingly, after some time, one teacher wanted us all to go to the sick room because she wanted us to see what was written on the wall. She had noted it was one name all over. Some older pupils recommended she show our class the writing.

We went to the room, and I noticed that Veronica and Lucy were standing in the back and laughing. They didn't take it seriously. I still tried to think good about people, especially about people whom I called my friends.

After some time, I talked to Caro to meet up again and sing together. She said, "No, I can't. Lucy is coming over." I was very confused because she had never been keen with her, but all of the sudden they acted like they had known each other for a long time.

After a while, Caro totally pushed me out of her life and

did everything with Lucy. I was sad and thought about the time Veronica and Lucy had spoken to her, because after that talk, everything changed.

Veronica still did a lot with me, and because I was still young, I didn't think anything bad would happen. This seemed normal with my best friends, and I didn't think of the way it could be behind my back.

When Lucy's birthday arrived each year, she always did a big party with her friends in her big house. She invited a lot of people from our class. It was a very nice party, and I liked the way everything was.

The evening after the party, almost everybody was gone except me and Veronica. Lucy came to me and said, "You have to leave now because just one can sleep here, and I want Veronica to sleep here, not you." Lucy had a very big bed in her room where four people could sleep inside, but still she wanted me to leave. Lucy and Veronica gave their evil smiles when my mum arrived to pick me up. When they were about to close the door, they said with a laugh, "Finally she is gone." That night I felt very sad, and I told my mum about it. She was shocked when she heard everything. She took me in her arms and tried to calm me down, but she could never erase it from my mind.

After a few weeks, my grades were getting worse because Veronica wasn't supporting me anymore and giving me confidence to speak up. I depended on her even though I knew that was wrong, but I couldn't stop it. I felt left out, like everything was falling apart. I felt pain in my heart that Veronica had left me, and Lucy had the power to take her over in the same way as with Caro. Lucy took everyone I was close to. I couldn't understand what power Lucy had over everybody and what she would tell them to turn against me in a second. But even though a lot of shit things happened, in some ways things were OK, at least when I was alone with any one of them.

After almost two years, somehow I got through it even with all the really hurtful sentences on the wall and still feeling left out of the group. Veronica told us that she had to change schools because her grades went down, so she decided to go to one of the lower schools.

My mum and I had already thought about it for a long time because my grades started to get really bad again. Too much was going on in my mind, and I couldn't really focus on school anymore. I decided to go with Veronica.

My mum had noticed my face over time, and I wasn't happy anymore. I talked to my mum and told her everything. My mum couldn't believe it and was very shocked to hear everything that was going on in school. She could not believe that they would actually write those things on the wall. My parents were always there for me, although sometimes my dad said that I had to get through it and shouldn't make it that big of a deal. I loved my parents from the bottom of my heart and appreciated everything they did for me.

One day I had a small operation on my tooth during school time because I had a lot of pain. When I arrived home after surgery, one of my main teachers called and shouted at my mum that I should come to school for the German exam. Meanwhile, my mum fought with her on the telephone. I was bleeding unexpectedly, and it was heavy. When my mum noticed it, she shouted at the teacher, "I need to go—my daughter is sick and bleeding. I don't have time for your stupid drama." After that, my mum and I went to the surgery again so they could calm it down.

That is what parents are for: they fight battles for you that you wouldn't even see. Always appreciate your parents no matter what happens, because they are the ones who will always fight for you and be by your side in every situation.

Even in that situation, no friend was there for me; they didn't even ask for me or call. I didn't want to believe or see the truth about my situation with my so-called best friends because every time I was alone with Lucy or Veronica, things seemed normal to me. Sadly, Caro was not there for me anymore. The second we were all together, I got left out, and they would tell me what I should do so they didn't have to do it. I didn't have enough confidence to say no, and I still tried to see the light at the end of the tunnel. It felt like I had confidence only when I was with Veronica but not by myself.

Finally, the time came when Lucy and Caro stayed at the first school, and Veronica and I changed to the lower school together. I was so happy that I had my best friend back. We were alone, just me and her. All I wanted was a new start with Veronica without Lucy being between them.

CHAPTER 3

HAPPINESS

It was a blessing when Veronica and I changed schools together. My parents and I were so relieved. I smiled big because we even got in the same class and were able to sit together.

Everybody was so nice to each other, and students welcomed us in a very friendly way. All of them talked to us, made jokes with us, and showed us the whole school.

I loved it there, and even the teachers were really friendly. We finally had our new start and could get closer, like before. We made a lot of good new friendships. We laughed every single day and enjoyed every day in school. That time, Veronica and I were very good in school. We had very good grades and were the most popular girls in school. Everybody wanted to be with us.

I got close with one girl named Amanda. She was very lovely and invited me to her house. We laughed, made videos together, and had so much fun. We even had sleepovers and tried to practice for exams together.

Veronica and I were still so close like never before. It felt like she was my sister from another mother.

One day, a boy named Max had to repeat the lower class

and came to ours. He was very popular. Every girl wanted him, but he never showed any interest to anybody, though he was friendly to everybody.

Veronica came to me one time and said, "You know, the new boy likes you very much."

I was surprised and said, "Well, that's good for him," and laughed. He was very nice to me at that time, helped me through some classes I had difficulties with, and was very supported towards me. I liked him, but just as a friend.

One day, one of my friends from school had a birthday party, and that time I colored my under hair black. I didn't know what I was thinking, but I wanted to try it because my friend Amanda had done the same thing. I said to myself, "Why not?" Everybody loved it, and I had so much confidence and laughed with everybody. Some people got the same hair style after they saw it on me.

That birthday party was really nice, and we had a lot of food and played games.

We got really close, and I enjoyed all the attention.

Veronica and I were a very good team together. Lucy was still there but was not in our school. They still met up sometimes but not as often as before. I also met up with Lucy because of our dance classes, but that was all. We had different friend circles now. She wasn't there in the school with us, so everything was fine.

It was such a great time, and I was confident that nothing would ever change it. I was never good in maths, so I wouldn't care about my maths grade because our teacher was really strange towards me and Veronica. He didn't really liked us. I could see it on his face, the way he looked at us every day. But by that time, I was very confident in myself and took it the way it was. I was good in other subjects, and that was enough for me. Even in some classes where I had never been good before, I now had the best grades.

After some months of school, we had summer holidays coming. That was when Veronica and I decided to do a English course to Spain for two weeks, so we could learn better English and still enjoy some sun. Our parents agreed, and we booked the flight and the course. We couldn't wait until we would have our first trip on a plane without our parents. We hoped to meet some new friends.

As the day arrived, we were so nervous and happy at the same time that we couldn't sleep the night before. We met up at the airport and met some other kids and the teachers for that course. They were very friendly, and everybody was open with each other. I was happy to do this trip with my best friend.

When we arrived, we met some other kids who were already there. We met at one point at the airport and then got into buses that transferred us to our temporary family. Veronica and I were in the same family. We had a lovely woman who had done it before two times with other girls. She welcomed us and made food for us when we arrived. We loved our room and bed, which was comfy, and she was friendly and welcoming.

Later that day, we had to do our first welcome class. Everybody had to introduce themselves. There were ten other kids, and all of them came from another town. They told us that we also had some free time in the evening, so we could enjoy some time at a restaurant or the beach with our friends. It was perfect.

Veronica already had her eye on one boy, Max. She liked

him, but that time she did have a boyfriend. So she refused to do more than she should do.

In the evening, we went home and ate with the woman, and after that we went to our bedroom to get some rest. We talked almost the whole night and planned what we should wear tomorrow, because it was very hot in Spain.

The next morning, we woke up, ate some breakfast, and walked to the town to meet everybody for our first English class. We were separated into two groups. There was an advanced class and than the one that had just started.

Veronica and I were in the advanced class. One girl immediately sat next to us and started talking. Her name was Emma. She was a kind, shy, cute, and friendly girl. Her eyes were light blue, and shewasvery pretty.

After the classes were finished, we all went for lunch together. We had a great time in our group. After lunch, Veronica and I went home and changed our dresses because we wanted to see the city.

Later that day, we met up with our group, wandered around the city, did some shopping, and enjoyed the beach. One boy came to me that day while Veronica was standing next to me and said, "You have such lovely eyes. Very bright." I smiled and thanked him.

Veronica was slightly smiling, but I felt that smile wasn't real. Night came, and we went to try some sushi. I had never tried it before, but I had always wondered how it would taste. Now I could say that I would never eat it again. Veronica loved it, but I couldn't get it down and ordered some fries.

Time passed fast, and we had to return to our houses. We went home in silence this time, ate something small, and went to our bedroom. When I lay in my bed, I heard some noises from the bathroom and saw that Veronica wasn't in her bed. I checked up because I was worried about her. As I stood by the door, I heard a strange noise. She was vomiting. She had put her finger in her throat.

I couldn't believe it and asked myself why she would do this. To me, she was pretty in every way. When she came out of the bathroom, I asked if everything was OK. She said, "Yes, just bad a stomach."

We looked at each other and went straight to sleep. The next morning, I wanted to talk to her about it, but she always pushed me away from that subject. It was clear she had a problem but didn't want to talk about it. I gave her some distance and didn't ask again.

During the day, everything was normal. We went to our course, met up with our friends, and enjoyed the sun and the time together. We played a lot of games and went for a swim.

Later that day, it was almost evening, and Veronica said, "I will go to Leo's place to hang out a bit, but you can go home. I will meet you there."

I looked at her and asked, "Are you sure?" She simply nodded. I thought for a moment and walked away. It was very strange because we never did anything apart, but all of the sudden she wanted to go alone to his place.

In the meantime, I walked home and met Emma on my way back home. She did not live far away from us, so she walked with me. We had a nice chat about a lot of things. We exchanged our numbers and stayed in contact that evening.

When Veronica came home, we had dinner together with the woman, and after we finished, we went to our room. I looked at her and said, "Do you want to talk about it?"

She stared at me and said, "What do we have to talk about? I just wanted some time alone." I tried to smile at her.

Later that evening, we went to bed, and again after some time, I heard her in the bathroom doing the same thing as the night before. I was very worried about her because she was perfect the way she was. Why would she do this to herself? I always saw her as my role model. I didn't say anything when she came back and went straight to bed because she told me not to worry.

The next morning, as always we went to our English course. The whole walk, she was on her phone texting, so I asked her if she had a good time yesterday. She said, "Yes, of course."

When we arrived, Emma came over and started talking to me. I was happy she did because I felt very bad about Veronica and what was happening. That day, our teachers said that we could have some free time and should enjoy the day, so we all went out to eat and enjoy ourselves. Veronica didn't sit next to me anymore, but I was OK with it as long as I knew we would be OK.

One boy, named Alex, talked to me again and asked me how I could have such beautiful eyes. I smiled in reply. That time I saw that Veronica look at me, and she seemed angry. I went to her and asked if everything was all right, and she answered, "Your eyes are not as beautiful as he said."

I frowned. "Why are you jealous because someone said I have nice eyes?" She turned away and whispered, "I am not jealous of you. how can I be?" It was getting late, so we all had to go home, but I couldn't find Veronica anywhere and couldn't reach her. I was worried something happened, until

Alex came to me and said that she had gone to the beach with Leo, so I should go home without her.

I was so confused as to why she wouldn't tell me by herself. I went home with Emma and talked to her about it. She was just as shocked as I was. She had had the feeling Veronica and I were close and that nothing would ever happen between us.

When I reached home, I tried to explain to the woman who took care of us that Veronica would come later, because she wanted to go and see the beach again. The woman said, "Well, then let's have a small dinner together." She was very friendly to me.

After some time, I went to the bedroom and to my bed. She didn't write me anything until then. I tried to sleep but couldn't really stop thinking about what had happened.

Veronica came back very late that night. She went straight to the bathroom and then to bed. She didn't even say anything. I knew that time something was going on, but she wouldn't speak to me.

On the last day of our trip, we the class made a sightseeing trip together, and we saw the whole city. It was really nice, and I enjoyed it. As the evening came, Veronica and I went home together this time and had a nice, long dinner with the woman. She talked to us about her previous girls and smiled the whole time. I told her that we really enjoyed staying with her, and hopefully we would see her again.

After dinner, we went to our bedroom and packed our bag. Veronica looked at me and said, "I am sorry I was so mean." I told her that it was OK and she shouldn't worry about it anymore.

The day arrived that we had to leave. We gave the

woman a big hug and left the house to our bus, which waited for everybody to come out. When we arrived at the airport, one teacher said that we had to go our separate ways on the second flight because some had to go to other cities. We all OK with it because some friends were still flying with us due to living near our city.

When we arrived at the transfer airport, one of the flight attendants said that the next flight to our city was overbooked, so they hoped they could fit everybody inside who needed to go.

I didn't really worry about it until we went to the gate. Veronica went in without turning to me. I was waiting to get in, and all of a sudden, one of the women said that the flight was full. I was shocked and wanted to cry. One friend who was still there with me waited and sat down next to me. He was allowed to go in after a few minutes, but I still had to wait. I was so shocked I couldn't think straight. Veronica didn't even care; I could hear her laughing and not caring about whether I would fly. After some time, I was relieved when the flight attendant said they had a seat for me. I went inside, looked around, and saw Veronica. She stared at me with a straight face. The whole flight, I wondered what had just happened and why Veronica wouldn't even care about me coming home with her.

After an hour-long flight, we arrived and saw our parents. Our parents spoke to each other and smiled when they saw us. When her parents said that they needed to go, Veronica looked away and didn't even say goodbye to me.

My mum looked at me asked if everything was all right. I replied, "Yes, I think." When we reached home, I couldn't hold it back and told my mum everything. She looked very confused and was shocked that Veronica would do this. Everything had seemed all right when we had left to Spain. She tried to calm me down and said that maybe Veronica was just tired and wanted to go home. I tried to calm down and didn't make a big deal out of it.

The next two days, I didn't hear anything from her—no phone calls and no text messages.

Monday arrived, and we had to go back to school. I thought at least there, I could speak to her and ask her if everything was OK with us.

When I saw her, she kept some distant from me. She wasn't as open to me as usual. We still sat next to each other but didn't really talk. It was very different, and I didn't know why. I tried to talk to her, but she didn't really reply to me.

When we were on our first big break, I saw Lucy walking towards us. I was very surprised because she didn't go to our school. I looked at Veronica, and she smiled at her and then ran towards her. They hugged each other and jumped up and down.

Lucy came to me and said, "I am going here now too."

I was shocked and said, "Oh, I didn't know you were coming here. No one told me."

She smiled at Veronica and said, "I told only the important people in my life." My body froze, and I couldn't move. I didn't want to believe it was true. After that, they walked away from me hand in hand like I didn't even exist. Luckily, Lucy didn't get a space in our class. I was relieved when I heard that because I wouldn't have been able to stand her in my class again.

Lucy soon made friends with two girls, Amelia and Sophia. Because she had them and didn't go to my class,

Veronica and I were getting along again. But there was always a feeling something wasn't right.

Sometimes in the breaks, I could see Veronica, Lucy, Amelia, and Sophia walking away without waiting for me.

When I found them, Lucy always smiled and said, "Oh, did we forget you?" I was concerned about how Lucy treated me when she came to our school because I couldn't believe she hadn't told me anything.

As the days passed, everything seemed normal as usual. We still had a lot of fun during class and had good grades.

Then one day, our main teacher came to us and said, "We have to separate the two classes into three, because we have too many pupils." I immediately thought about Lucy. I did not want her in my class again to destroy everything I had with Veronica.

The teachers said they would give us up to two weeks, so we had time to choose with whom we wanted to be in the same class.

I wanted to write down only Veronica, but she saw and pushed me to write Lucy too. I did it eventually and saw that she wrote down me and Lucy. She said she wanted us three to be together.

I was very nervous because I didn't want this to happen. I had a feeling it would end badly again. I knew when we would be together in class again, they would push me aside and would do everything together—without me.

After we wrote the names down, immediately Lucy came to us and said, "Oh, I am so happy. Maybe we can be together again." She looked at me, smiled, and added, "Sorry, but I forgot to write your name down. I wrote Amelia." Then she walked away.

I looked at Veronica, and she shrugged like she didn't care. I felt so confused and asked myself what I had done to Lucy that she treated me like crap.

I didn't deserve it. She had come down to our school because she wanted to be with Veronica, and she couldn't stand that I was with her. What friend would treat a best friend the way Lucy treated me?

CHAPTER 4

INNOCENT

The two weeks passed too quickly. I was so nervous and hoped Lucy wouldn't be in the same class as me and Veronica. I prayed, "Please, God, not again."

The next morning arrived, and our teacher had the list that would change my life. She said all the names for the first class and the second, but my, Veronica's, and Lucy's names weren't on that list. I knew we would be in the same class. And I was right: in the next moment, our teacher listed the names for the third class. "Amelia, Sophia, Lucy, Veronica, and Delilah," she said at last. Veronica was very happy and looked at me with a big smile on her face. During the break, Lucy, Amelia, Veronica, and Sophia met up and hugged each other. After a while they saw me and hugged me, but it was because they had to, not because they wanted to.

After a long, terrible school day, I went home with my bike. While I rode my bike, I heard some music. Music always made me more calm, like I was in a moment and no one could destroy that special moment.

When I reached home, I couldn't think straight. I went to my mum and told her that I would be in class with Lucy again.

She looked at me and said, "Maybe this time it will be different. You never know. Just know you are the light—and stand up for yourself."

I nodded at my mum. She was right, but it was hard to actually do it. Especially when I was not the loudest. I didn't have enough confidence to actually stand up for myself in front of anybody.

After lunch, I went upstairs to my room and heard some music. I tried to relax and to not allow any negative thoughts about all this school drama.

The next day, I woke up, ate breakfast, and went to school. When I arrived at school, I immediately saw Lucy walking to the entrance with Veronica by her side. In that second, I felt lost, scared, and vulnerable.

Before I went in, Amelia, who was now also in my class, came towards me and went upstairs next to me. We talked about dance and some music. She was really nice and open to me that time.

When we came inside the classroom, I saw that Lucy and Veronica had already chosen their seats without me. They sat next to each other and didn't even look at me once. Amelia came to me and said, "You can sit next to me and Sophia."

I looked at her and thanked her. I was glad she had made a step towards me, or else I wouldn't know where to sit. I didn't know anybody else well in that class.

The first day in the new classroom, with new pupils and a new teacher. It was not the same anymore. I knew I had to eventually adapt to it, but the way it was it was not right.

Veronica came to me during one small break and said, "Why didn't you come earlier so you could sit next to me?"

I stared at her and said, "I do not want to be next to Lucy too. But don't worry, it's fine."

She went back to Lucy, and they immediately started chatting. I believed it was about me, and I think I was right, because they whispered and looked at me like I was an alien.

I felt so innocent and small. I hadn't done anything wrong, but I felt like I did everything wrong.

Later that day, I thought that I should have said that Veronica could have held the space for me while I wasn't in school. But I couldn't do it. I was not strong enough to say anything to her.

After our lunch break, Amelia came to me and told me that she didn't live far from my place. I was surprised and asked her where she lived.

She told me and directed me to her place after school. That day Amelia told me that she would like to have some meet-ups with me so we could chat and do some things together.

I was so happy in that moment that someone had thought of me and wanted to spend time with only me.

The next morning, I went to Amelia's house. It was a very nice place to live. We talked a lot that day also about Lucy and Veronica. She told me that she was always getting angry when Lucy said to her that she couldn't do something. Amelia said she didn't really like her that much because she was very bossy.

I was surprised when she told me all of that, and I couldn't believe what she said.

I asked her why she had done everything with her for the last few months.

"You know, the first time I met Lucy, she was really

nice. Sophia and I have been best friends since nursery. We all played nicely together for some time. But after a few months, Lucy said she didn't want Sophia with us anymore and told me that I should not talk to her again."

When I heard that, I answered, "I know how you feel, believe me."

After that, we talked about our hobbies. She loved dancing as much as I did. We started to do a dance video. We filmed it outside on the fields, on the streets, or in the house. Afterwards, she cut it and sent it to me so I could view it. I loved every single video we did.

After some weeks, we had maths. I wasn't good at maths, and this time our teacher was our headmaster. He didn't like any jokes. During class, our headmaster looked at me and asked about the answer for the question he had written on the board. I tried, but I couldn't answer it. Veronica raised her hand and answered the question correctly. Veronica and Lucy looked at me and laughed. „No Looser would know this." Veronica said proudly.

I felt so ashamed-empty, like I was nothing and didn't know anything. I wanted to sink into the ground. I remembered when Veronica supported me with everything, but now I didn't even get a proper hello from her in the morning.

After that class me, Lucy and Veronica went to buy some food. We always went to a bakery nearby to buy some fresh bread. We had to climb over a fence, and I hated it every time.

They both went in front of me and went over the fence. I couldn't really get over it because my leg started hurting me.

Lucy and Veronica looked at me bored, and Lucy said,

"Are you too fat to get over?" Then they just went away without me.

I wanted to cry because I didn't deserve this, but I believed I couldn't do anything about it. I was always nice to her and Veronica, and I tried my best to be there for everybody. I blamed myself that I wasn't strong enough to say, "Fuck you, you ugly snake," and stand up for myself.

I just couldn't do it, and I always blamed it on the way she treated me every day. I just let it happen, like they could do anything with me and I would still stand by their side.

After that, I went to the classroom and sat down. I didn't want to go out and stand alone somewhere. Amelia and Sophia came to me after a while. I didn't tell them what was going on and talked to them about something else.

Amelia told me that there was a new dance school open she wanted to try with me. She thought it would be a good move to try it out. At that time, I didn't know she was also friends with Anita from my old ballet class, because she mentioned she knew the school from her. More of that later.

I replied that I would love to come with her.

As the next lesson started, Lucy and Veronica came in just before the bell. They looked at me and made a laugh and sad face, and then they started laughing out loud and sat down.

I wanted to go home and go to my bed. That lesson, I couldn't really concentrate.

I got distracted every time Veronica or Lucy laughed because I thought it was always because of me. I felt uncomfortable and wanted to cry.

Lucy came to me after class and mentioned the dance school as well, because she wanted to try it out. They had more dance styles available. She told me and stared at me for a moment to see my reaction.

I replied, "Amelia asked me to come and see how it is." She smiled and said that she would be happy to see me there.

That time I became really confused. Why would she say this, but in the next minute she would treat me like crap?

After the school day was over, I went to Amelia's place, and we both went to the new dance school in town. I saw Anita and Lucy already standing there, waiting for us. We went in and took our first hip-hop class together. I loved it, because it was so nice and I could be myself.

Lucy didn't really like it and was much happier with ballet.

I also wanted to continue ballet, so I went with Lucy and Anita the next day to the ballet class. I did like it, but with Lucy and Anita, it was just like before when we were younger. I wanted to keep dancing, so I had to get used to it. At least I was lucky that I had the hip-hop class without Lucy.

For the next vacation period, we decided to have a sleepover together. Veronica, Lucy, Sophia, Amelia, and I got together. Amelia's mother worked late one evening, so we decided to sleep at Amelia's house.

We went to her place and had a lovely day, and as the evening arrived, we ordered some pizza for us.

After we ate, we went outside and enjoyed the warm night. We did some pictures together and posted them. After a moment, Lucy took out a cigarette. She lit it up and inhaled the smoke deeply into her lungs. We looked at her, and then Veronica laughed and took one as well. Everybody did it except me that night. They tried to push me to do it, but I didn't want to. Lucy said, "Are you a loser?" I looked at her and took one breath with the cigarette, but I intensely drank some water, and I didn't do it again. I hated it.

The sun rose, and we ate some breakfast together. We talked about a lot of things and agreed that it was good to have friends like us. After some time, everybody went home except me. I helped Amelia clean up the house so she didn't have to do it alone.

When we finished, I went home with my bike and tried to get some sleep. We had some more sleepovers, but not with everybody; sometimes it was just me and

Amelia, Lucy and Veronica often wantedtodo something alone.

I was happy when I had some time apart from Lucy and Veronica. I enjoyed the time with Amelia or Sophia.

The day before our first day back at school, I felt so nervous and scared to go back. I didn't see Veronica or Lucy again during the break after that sleepover together. They didn't even write or call.

Monday came, and I woke up and went straight to school. When I arrived at school, I saw Veronica and Lucy standing at a side entrance, smoking. I couldn't believe my eyes, I thought that what had happened at the sleepover was just once, but I was very wrong.

They stood with some older pupils from our school. When they saw me passing them with my bike, they smiled, but the second after I passed, they turned to the older pupils and laughed.

I knew that this day wouldn't be an easy day. When the first class started, I sat down next to Amelia, and we talked about the homework we had to do.

I saw Veronica and Lucy behind me, laughing. They looked at me and gestured to my hair.

I touched my hair and felt something sticky in my hair. It was gum. When I tried to pull it out, Veronica and Lucy laughed. Amelia tried to pull it out, with success. I felt so ashamed at that time. After that class, I went to the bathroom to clean up my hair a bit more. Lucy and Veronica came after me and started to pull on my hair. "You still have something in your ugly hair. You had better clean it up, or it will stink—like you," they said.

The second they left, I started crying. I tried to keep it inside but couldn't. After some minutes, I went out and started walking to our classroom. At that moment, I saw my teacher we had in my first class. She looked at me and asked if everything was OK. I nodded at her and went upstairs to the classroom. I sat down and didn't say or do anything.

When I came home, my parents both looked at me and saw that I wasn't happy. I told them what had happened, and my dad replied, "Get over it. Don't make a big deal out of it. You need to be strong."

I was lost. "So it was all my fault—what they did? They didn't do anything wrong to me?" My dad turned around and walked away from me and my mum. My mum looked at me and gave me a tight hug. I couldn't say anything in that moment and just wanted to be held.

In the afternoon, Amelia and I had our hip-hop lesson. We went to Amelia's place and had some lunch. I didn't tell her anything about what had happened in the bathroom. We talked about other stuff and what we should wear to the dance class.

The time came, and we rode our bikes to the dance

school and met Anita. We went inside the room, and just wanted to focus on that class. I tried not to think about anything else that was going on in school.

After some quiet weeks in school, Sophia, Veronica, Lucy, and I got a text message that Amelia was sick and had to go to hospital. She had to stay there for at least two weeks to get better. I was very worried when I read that message because she was always so healthy. I hoped that she would get better quickly.

In the break, Veronica, Lucy, Sophia, and I met up and talked about the text message. We were very concerned but had to wait until her mother or Amelia would reply about what was going on.

That week, Sophia and I became closer, and we had some meet-ups and had a lot of fun together. I tried to distract her from what was going on with Amelia, because they were best friends.

She was very open to me at that time, and she told me how she felt. She was happy that I was good company. I said, "That is what friends are for," and hugged her.

After the week passed, Veronica and Lucy kept quiet, but not entirely quiet. One day they posted a picture of me, Lucy, and Veronica on the internet. I read some of the comments, and people were saying things like, "Who is that little ugly girl in the middle?"

Veronica replied, "No one important."

I looked through and was sad to read all the shit comments about me. Veronica or Lucy also commented things like that. Then why did they post it in the first place?

Every Thursday, I went to the dance class with Anita and tried to focus on that more than anything else. I loved the hip-hop class, and it felt really good. After some time I got a reply from Amelia, saying, "Hey, Delilah. I will be home in a few days. I feel much better. Just wanted to let you know. Love you." I smiled at the message and called Sophia. She was even happier than I was, and we couldn't wait for Amelia to return.

When Amelia returned, something changed. The day she was back, she sat next to Lucy and Veronica in class, not next to me. She said hello to me but nothing more. Sophia also turned to Amelia now and totally ignored me.

I sat alone in my seat, with no friends.

When the break came, everybody went out. Veronica, Lucy, Amelia, and Sophia left without me. They didn't seem to care about me. They left the classroom and went to the bakery without me.

I was alone during every break and felt lost. I asked myself what I was supposed to do. Was I wrong? Did I do something to them that I couldn't remember?

I sat down on a bench and saw Max coming to me. He smiled and made small talk with me. I was happy he talked to me because I felt ashamed to sit alone during a break.

During class, they still ignored me when I tried talking to them. They continued their conversation like I was a ghost. Finally, the school day finished, and I went home alone. I ate some lunch and went straight to my room. My mum noted me being unhappy, so she came to my room and talked to me.

I told her what had happened, and she gave me a big hug. "Do you want to do something about it? How are your grades? Do you want me to talk to their parents?"

I said that I didn't want her to talk to them. Maybe it was just that day, and it would get back to normal soon.

Two days later, during a small break, I went to the bathroom. I locked the door, and all I could hear from the outside was laughter from some girls. They sounded like Veronica, Lucy, Amelia, and Sophia. When I washed my hands and wanted to go out, they came in and pushed me on the ground. After that, they ran out and held the door so I couldn't get out.

I screamed and begged them to open it up. After some time, a teacher came, immediately took them away, and opened the door. The laughed at me and ran away. The teacher looked at me and asked me if everything was all right. I just said yes and walked away.

I had to hold back my tears that time because I didn't want to make them see how hurt I was.

After that incident, I went to the headmaster and said that I wasn't feeling well and wanted to go home. He looked at me and agreed. I went home and ran to my bed. My mum came upstairs and asked me what had happened and why I was home already.

I lied that I wasn't feeling well, and I didn't want to go to school tomorrow.

She looked at me very shocked and didn't know what to say. After some time, she left my room, and I started crying. I didn't want to tell her because she was already worried about me, so I didn't want to put more on her.

The next day, I had to go back, but I didn't want to. I was so terrified to go back to the classroom and to sit alone.

Every time I stepped on the school grounds, I started shaking and couldn't breathe. My heart stopped, and I wanted to cry. I couldn't be sure that it wouldn't happen again.

That day, Veronica came to me and talked surprisingly normal to me, but when Lucy came around the corner, she stepped away from me. Lucy smiled at me and said, "Did you cry enough now?"

I wanted to be strong and tried to walk away from them. I went upstairs and sat down in my seat.

During the small break, I had to use the bathroom but was terrified to go inside. I always waited until someone else was inside so that I wouldn't be alone inside.

That day at one lesson, we had to move some tables, including mine. I tried to put my things from the ground onto the table. My head was under one table, and I saw Lucy push my table and say, "Hurry up." She didn't wait, and I knocked my head on the side from the table. I felt so much pain, but she smiled and went back to her seat. Our teacher looked at me and asked me if I needed help. I shook my head and got back up.

Veronica, Amelia, Sophia, and Lucy hid their smiles, but I could see them clearly behind their fake masks.

When I came back home that day, I went to my mum and said, "I can't do it anymore. I don't want to go back to school. I am alone, and no one is by my side."

My mum gave me a big hug. She asked what I thought about changing the class. Because there were three classes, I could try to get to the one where my first teacher was teaching. Maybe I would find some support with her.

I had to think because I didn't want to let Veronica or Lucy feel that I was running away from them. Even now, I felt that they would be still my friends.

When I went to school the next day, my former teacher from the other class spoke to me. "How are you feeling today? Is everything going well in your class? I heard that you seem distracted during class." I looked down and nodded my head. I told her that Veronica and Lucy weren't as nice to me anymore as they used to be, and that I felt alone because I didn't have anybody to rely on.

She said, "Why don't you come to my class? There is still one space."

I told her that I would think about it, even though my mum told me to do it. But I needed some time because I didn't want to see the reality about my friendship with my best friends.

When I went back to my classroom, I was about to sit, but all of a sudden I felt on the ground. Lucy took my chair away so that I felt on the ground. Everybody laughed and gestured towards me. I ran out of class and to the bathroom and started crying. That time, I knew that I needed to get out of there, even if it was just to the other class.

After school, I went home and told my mum that I wanted to change to the other class. She nodded and immediately called the school. To my surprise, the headmaster agreed, and I was able to go to that class the next week.

That week, I tried to not talk about anyone, and the headmaster didn't speak to anyone from the class either. He did see that something was going on and didn't want to make it worse for me.

Wednesday came, and I had my ballet class. Lucy was also there with Anita. They didn't say hello or even look at me. If they did look at me, they simply laughed. When I was supposed to show one exercise in the middle of the room, Anita and Lucy made fun of me.

I tried to ignore them, but it wasn't easy at all.

When ballet class finished, I asked Anita if we would go the hip-hop class together tomorrow. She looked at me quiet arrogantly and said, "I would never go with you." Then she walked away.

I felt hurt, sad, and alone. Why would she also turn against me? I had never done anything to her.

In the evening, I got a message from Anita saying, "Hey, we can go together tomorrow. Meet you at the old place."

When I read that, I was surprised but accepted it.

During school break the next day, I sat down alone on a bench next to a sand place. Some from my old class came to me and talked to me for a while before moving on to their classroom.

As I went to my classroom, Lucy came behind me and pushed me down. I laid there for a minute and couldn't move. I was in shock at what had just happened. She ran away with Veronica and Amelia and laughed so loud one could hear it everywhere.

In that moment, one pupil from the other class came and helped me up. She looked at me concerned and walked with me. I was glad someone was there and helped me in that moment. I thanked her, and we headed to our classroom.

In that class, I couldn't focus on anything. I simply wanted the week to end now so I could go to my new class and move on with my life.

I couldn't stand Lucy or Veronica's sight anymore. Even though Veronica tried to talk to me sometimes, the minute

Lucy was coming, Veronica would ignore me again and push me aside.

After school, I went straight to my room. I listened to music for hours. I prayed that this week would be over soon and that everything would be all right. I lay down for a few hours, tried to relax, and heard some good music. I didn't think of anything else and tried to push myself through this week until I was free to go to the other class. It was hard to go to class every day until next week. I even asked my mum to let me stay home, but she wouldn't agree to that.

The last day I went to that class, I tried to ignore everyone who had laughed at me the other day. When I came in the room, everybody looked at me. Some laughed and some ignored me.

Veronica came to me and asked if it was true that I would leave the class. I looked at her and asked where she had heard that. She said someone from class overheard their teacher saying that I would leave to the second class because of some difficulties. I didn't say anything for some minutes but eventually said, "Yes, I will go," and I sat down.

During the break, everybody looked at me like I had done something very wrong and they were all innocent.

Lucy came to me and said, "Why would you go? You think you will be better in the other class?" She laughed in my face. I ignored it and moved away from her. Amelia and Sophia looked at me during the break but didn't say anything. I think they knew why I would change classes, but they wouldn't say anything else.

The last lesson passed quickly, and one girl named Anna came up to me and said, "I hope you will be OK in the other class. I have seen what Lucy and her friends do to you." I tried to smile at her and sat down.

When the class finished, I went outside and saw that Lucy and Veronica behind me. Then I felt a push, I fell down four steps in the school hall and couldn't stand up for some minutes.

Lucy stared at me. "You have a problem?" she asked. Then she took Veronica by her arm and went outside.

I looked everywhere for my bike but couldn't find it. I knew I had locked it and put it in the bike hall, but it was nowhere to be found. When I walked outside the bike hall, I saw my bike damaged and lying on the ground in the bushes. I saw Lucy, Veronica, Amelia, and Sophia at the opposite side of the hall, laughing and running away. I picked up my bike up and had to walk it home because my wheels were damaged.

When I arrived home, my mum saw my bike and wondered where I was because it was very late for me to get home. I told her everything. She looked at my bike and said, "It will be all right."

I went to my grandfather's house and asked him to fix my bike for me. He immediately fixed it so I could ride it the next week.

I wasn't sure whether I was happy or sad. I would still see my old classmates during the break or after school, but I was relieved I didn't have to tolerate them during class anymore.

During the weekend, I posted a picture of me on my Facebook page. I saw that Veronica commented under it, so I checked it. Her comment said, "How did you get the fat pimple under your eyebrow? And what's wrong with your hair?" Lucy said under one photo, "Hey, my ugly friend," with a kiss smiley. I deleted the picture immediately because I couldn't stand the comments from any of them. Why couldn't they just shut the fuck up? Why didn't they manage their lives and leave me to manage mine? They couldn't let me be. Why?

CHAPTER 5

ALONE

Finally the next week arrived, and I went to my new class. I met the main teacher in front of the headmaster office, and she took me with her to the new classroom. She told me that I shouldn't worry about anything and that everything would be fine.

I was very nervous but excited at the same time. I was excited about the new classmates I would meet, and I was relieved that I was able to change the class. I finally had a fresh new start.

The moment I came into the class, everybody stared at me but smiled. One girl came to me and said that I could sit next to her and her friend. Their names were Liza and Megan.

I had a big smile on my face and sat down immediately. They told me what they were learning in this lesson and tried to show me everything they had done. It was similar to my last class. Everybody was so friendly to me, came up to me, and introduced themselves.

After class, we had a small break, and everybody sat down and talked about school and hobbies. One boy, Mike, spoke to me and said that if I needed help in math or history,

I could ask him. I thanked him and went back to my seat as the bell rang again.

The minute I sat down, I felt free. Finally no one laughed or teased me behind my back. My body was so relieved from the lack of stress, which I had been internalizing the past few months.

On the first big break, I saw Veronica, Lucy, Amelia, and Sophia walking past me. Lucy had her arrogant look towards me, and Veronica tried to smile small but then took Lucy's arm, like they wanted to show me that they didn't need me at all. I tried to ignore it and moved on.

Liza asked me to come with her to get something to eat. We sat down and talked. Along came Amelia and Megan. We sat together for the break and laughed the whole time. It was the first time in months that I could laugh from my heart. Finally I felt like I mattered. I hadn't had that feeling in a very long time.

After the break, we went upstairs to our classroom. The new classroom was on the opposite side of my old classroom, so eventually I would see Veronica and Lucy. I always tried to run as fast as possible so I wouldn't see anybody. When I met them in the morning, Veronica and Amelia always said good morning to me but didn't want to make it too obvious. Lucy had her evil smile every time she saw me. I could see in her face that she had something in her mind again— something evil.

Liza and I got along pretty well. We had a lot to talk about every day and had so much fun together. She stood by my side every day and helped me in school like Veronica had in the first months. I wasn't really scared to get closer with someone again because I didn't believe everybody would be like Lucy, Veronica, or Amelia, changing in one minute against me for no good reason. I also had Nicola during this time, and she didn't leave me for anything. That was why I knew there were still good people in this world.

When we had our sports class that day, we had football, and I hated it. Liza, Megan, Ava, and I were in one group, and I was in the goal. As they played towards me, I ran out of the goal to the side. Everybody laughed, including me, because I was scared of footballs. Eventually our teacher changed the formation for me, but it was a good laugh for everyone. It felt so good to laugh with others and not to be laughed at.

We always made a lot of jokes about everything that was going on. We tried to have some fun in class, even when it was hard or we should have been concentrating more. It was a really nice feeling to laugh out loud again and to not be blamed for everything that happened.

I loved being around Liza, and she made me feel strong again. The first time we met up, I went to her place because it wasn't too far from our school. We always went with our bikes to school. Every morning I picked her up, and we went with Mike as well.

I went to her house often, and we bonded. We watched movies, made pizza, and made some funny videos of ourselves. We enjoyed each other's company very much. We made each other laugh and happy, and I knew I could come to her when I had something on my mind that was worrying me.

One day on a small vacation, we had a meeting with Ava and Megan. We all went to Liza's house, cooked, made videos, and talked all night. In the evening, we built a tent.

It took some hours to build it, but it was perfect when it was done. We all slept inside because we heard noises from outside and got scared. But we laughed over it because we always made jokes. We claimed if someone would come, no one could do us harm because we were the power women in a tent.

When the sun rose, it was very early. It was 6:00 a.m. in the morning, when usually everybody was still sleep. We woke up and went inside the house to sleep in Liza's room some more.

After a few hours, we woke up, and it was 1:00 p.m. We went downstairs to eat some late breakfast. Her parents were already at work, so we had the house to ourselves. We watched TV, ate our food, and enjoyed some relaxing time together. When I went home, my mum saw my happy face, and I could see her smile. I went upstairs and took a shower. When I finished, I went to my room and saw all our pictures on Facebook. Liza had posted all of them, and they were ridiculously good. It was such a great feeling to be involved again in a group of friends. The next day, I went to a shop and printed all of them. I put them on my wall. I loved to see everybody happy the way we were that night. It was a really good feeling. The next day, Liza came to my house to have some time together, just us two. That day she asked me about Veronica and Lucy. She said that she had heard some rumors about me and them. I told her that a lot of things changed when Lucy came to our school and that the problem started when we had to change classes. It was like I was good for some times, when they needed someone to push aside, someone they could blame for everything. I always had the shortest stick, and I always had to do all the trashy things.

The minute Lucy befriended anybody, I was nothing to them anymore, and they wouldn't care about me again. I still didn't know what had happened with Amelia, because all of a sudden she liked Lucy more than anything, and she ignored me just like all the others.

Liza looked at me and said, "I am really sorry to hear that. The first time I saw Lucy, I knew I didn't want anything to do with her. She is something else. I can't even explain it, but I don't like her."

We decided to go out. We walked to one ice cream shop near my place. Suddenly, Liza saw Lucy, Veronica, and Amelia sitting on the bench, smoking next to the cafe. "Oh, hey, you. How are you? Did you find a nice friend now who believes your lies?" Lucy said, smiling.

Liza looked at me, stepped between me and Lucy, and said, "Shut up, you pig." After that, Liza and I walked away. We didn't get our ice cream, but we had a good laugh during our way home.

Lucy didn't reply when Liza said that to her. She was shocked that someone would actually say something mean to her. She couldn't even say anything and rolled her eyes at us.

I was so happy that someone had finally stood up for me and that I was not wrong about Lucy.

The next few months passed quickly. After that incident, we didn't hear a lot from Lucy, Veronica, or Amelia. They contacted me mainly over text message so no one could see what they said to me. Sometimes they sent me some text messages saying, "How can you even walk with your fat legs? Why is your face so ugly?

Hide it."

I had Liza, and she supported me during all this time. Of course, it did hurt to read those messages, but I got confident again and started to feel like myself. Liza always tried to push me up and said I should have more positive thoughts about life. She once said that I was really bright and shouldn't let anybody ruin things for me. She would be always here with me. That time she even called me her best friend and added that she was very happy that I had changed into her class.

I felt loved, wanted, and cared for. It was a great feeling to have a friend like her in my life again. I was good in class, had good grades, and behaved during lessons. I was one of the best pupils in our class.

One morning something changed. When I walked in class, Megan and Ava looked at me with a face I had never seen before on them. Liza appeared behind my back and hardly looked at me. That moment I knew something wasn't right.My heart started racing. I sat down next to Liza and started talking to her. She looked at me annoyed and said, "I don't want to talk now. Let me focus on my maths." I immediately turned the other way and focused on maths. After that class, Liza, Megan, and Ava walked out without me.

I thought I had a déjà vu and didn't know what was going on again. They left me out and forgot about me. What was it?

When I ran after them, they didn't wait for me. They grabbed some food and sat down on a bench. I sat down next to them and asked if anything was wrong. I wanted to know why they would act like this towards me.

They looked at me, and Liza finally said, "Ask yourself."

My heart felt heavy, and I felt like I was falling into a dark hole. I lost the ground under my feet and didn't know what had happened—again. What had I done? They stood up and walked away. Nearby, I saw Lucy and Veronica. They looked at me and laughed. Lucy came towards me and said, "What did you do again?" She smiled arrogantly.

I walked away and tried to figure out in my head what I had done. I couldn't think of anything because a few days ago, everything was fine.

After two days, I reached out to Liza and tried to talk to her in school, alone. I wanted her to tell me what was going on. Eventually, she sat down and started talking. "You know, Lucy told me that you lied about your illness and that it's not as bad as you told me. I just wonder why you would lie to me, because I thought we were friends, and I did worry about you."

I tried to explain it again and told her that she should google it if she didn't believe me. I just wanted us to be OK again. I emphasized that I didn't lie to her and couldn't believe she would actuallybelieve Lucy.

We were very quiet for a moment and didn't say anything. When she looked at me, she said, "I am sorry. I shouldn't have believed Lucy. You are right." She hugged me tight and apologized again.

I was glad that we were able to solve the problem so quickly and move ahead. After that discussion, I thought that everything was back to normal, but I was very, very wrong.

On the weekend, I didn't hear anything from Liza. That Saturday, I met up with Nicola and talked to her about it, because I needed someone to talk to.

She replied, "You know Lucy. She would do anything to destroy your friendship." I looked at her and knew that she was right, but couldn't believe that Liza would believe her, because she always told me she hated her.

After a few days, I wanted to pick up Liza from her home and go to school together. When I arrived, her mother opened the door and said that she had already left. I said to her other, "But she told me to pick her up." Her mother shrugged and closed the door.

I went to school alone. When I went to go upstairs to our classroom, I saw Veronica, Lucy, and Liza standing in the school hall, talking. When Liza saw me, she immediately cut short the conversation and went upstairs. I ran after her and shouted at her, "What was that all about? I thought you don't like them."

She replied, "Why do you care whom I like or not?" Then she went inside our classroom. At that moment, I heard Veronica and Lucy giggling behind my back. When I turned around, Lucy pushed me to the side. I knew she had said something false about me to Liza.

When I went inside and sat down next to Liza, Ava and Megan also stared at me and shook their heads. I tried to ignore it and focus on my class. I looked down on my paper, and in that lesson I didn't say or do anything again. I couldn't stop thinking about what had happened, and I wondered what Lucy had told Liza. I couldn't believe that she would actually believe Lucy over me. Just a few days ago, she had said that she was wrong to believe her. Now she stood up for Lucy again. Why?

I decided to talk to her in the small break again and find out what was going on.

When the bell rang, I wanted to confront her, but Megan and Ava took her and ran downstairs. I packed my things and tried not to cry. The moment I went out of my classroom, Veronica, Lucy, and Amelia stood at their classroom door. "Are you a crybaby?" they said.

I looked down and ran downstairs to the bathroom. I locked myself in for some minutes and didn't want to go back. When I came out, Liza stood in front of me. I looked at her and wanted to go out, but she held me back. "Lucy told me that you think that I am too ugly to ever get a boyfriend."

I shook my head and said that I never said that to her. I hadn't even spoken to Lucy or Veronica since I had changed classes. She told me she wasn't sure about who to believe again. I took her hand and emphasized that I would never lie to her, and it hurt me that she would believe Lucy and not me.

She just looked at me for some time and then went outside. I went after her, but she didn't wait.

We eventually went upstairs to our classroom and quietly sat down. I received a small paper, and something was written on it. It said, "Are you not ashamed to lie?" I looked around and saw Ava and Megan staring at me. I threw it away and tried to focus on my class again, but I got distracted pretty easy. I looked at Liza, but she ignored me the whole day. She didn't wait for me after school and went home. I was alone and vulnerable.

Mike waited for me to come, and we went home together. He talked to me and asked what was wrong, but I couldn't tell him because I wasn't sure what was really wrong. I had never lied to Liza.

When I reached home, my mum looked at me and asked about my day. I said, "Normal as always," and went upstairs to my room. I put on my music and tried to distract myself from everything. After some minutes, my phone made a noise. It was Liza texting me.

"I know you lied. Lucy told me again, and I believe her. How can you say this about me? I thought you were my friend. You should feel ashamed of yourself. Don't ever talk to me again."

I read the message and started crying, I couldn't believe Lucy had done it again. She took my friend, whom I liked very much, and made her believe that I was the bad one. I wanted to scream. I also wanted to punish myself. Now they made me believe I had actually done something wrong— and that I was always doing something wrong to lose friends.

Why did this always happen to me? I never did anything wrong to someone I liked. I always tried to support people in everything they did, and I was there for them when they needed it. They could always relay on me. I would have done everything for them. I was so tired of everything and felt so weak, because no one appreciated the effort I put in a friendship.

After some time, I went to my Facebook page and saw that Liza had deleted all our pictures and videos. I got frustrated and didn't know why this was happening again. I closed my computer and lay down on my bed.

I wanted to write and call her, but I couldn't because

I knew she wouldn't pick up, or she would block me everywhere.

She wouldn't let me explain or say anything that was against her beliefs. Liza believed Lucy—that was fact, and I couldn't do anything about it. I tried to do something in school, but she still believed Lucy and not me.

The next morning, I went to school and saw Lucy. Veronica, Liza, and Megan stood in the hall together. I tried to ignore them and wanted to walk upstairs to my classroom.

When I passed them, they said, "What is your problem, loser? No friends?" I looked away and ran upstairs as I heard them laughing behind my back. Suddenly a hand touched my shoulder. It was Mike. He saw everything and said that I should sit next to him. I immediately said yes and was very thankful. I took my stuff and sat down next to him. He talked to me and tried to make some jokes, but nothing helped. When our teacher arrived and saw me next to Mike, she looked at me and asked quietly if everything was all right. I just shook my head, and she nodded.

During class, I got a note that said, "So now you are running away like a baby." I looked over at Liza, and she laughed.

Mike read it, threw it away, and said, "Don't mind them."

It was easier said than done, but I tried my best. During the break, I stood alone in the school hall and ate my bread. Soon I saw some shadow behind me. It was Lucy. She looked down at me and threw my bread on the ground. I tried to clean it up, but she stepped on it and walked away to Veronica, Amelia, Sophia, Ava— and Liza. They stood in a small circle and laughed. I couldn't take it anymore, and I ran outside and sat on the bench next to our headmaster's office. After some time, two girls from my class approached me and said, "Why do you sit all alone here? I thought you are always with Liza." I simply shook my head. They took my hand and said, "Then come with us. We will go and get some food from the bakery."

I went with them to the bakery, and we started talking. I told them the short version of what had happened. They said that I shouldn't mind the others and move on, adding that eventually every storm calmed down.

When our sports lesson started, we had to choose a group of three or four. I looked around and was lost. I didn't have anybody again to do something with. Liza, Amelia, and Megan came over and said, "Sorry, we are full," and went away.

The two girls from earlier approached me again and said that I should do it with them. Their names were Gabriella and Luna. I tried to smile and went with them to a corner to figure out what we wanted to do. We had to choose from football, dance, and gymnastics. The three of us decided to do dance because we had all had dance lessons before, and I hadn't gone to my dance lesson in a long time.

During the week, we had to meet up and made a routine with a song. Meeting up with them took my mind away from everything that was going on. We practiced for about one week, and then it was our turn to show our routine and teach others how to do it. We had lots of fun together, but Liza, Megan, and Ava didn't even smile once. I tried to ignore them because I knew I was good at dancing, and everybody else thought so too. After class, our teacher came to us and congratulated us for completing the routine so well. She was very proud of us, and I was relieved we had it done so early.

After sports, we went down to our classroom. The moment I entered the stairs, I saw Veronica and Lucy going into one class downstairs. Everybody was inside that classroom. They left the door slightly open, and Veronica started yelling around the classroom that my family was a witch family. She made fun of me and my family the whole time. Everybody laughed and cheered her on. Why wouldn't they stop? And now they were even talking badly about my family!

When I went upstairs, I saw Mike waiting for me. He touched my shoulder and said, "It will be all right. I am here for you." I wanted to cry, go home, and never come back to this stupid school.

When the bell rang, everybody went to their classrooms. I sat down next to Mike and was quiet the whole day. I didn't want to do anything again. Those who had said they were my friends laughed and teased me behind my back. They ignored me when I passed them, and they pushed me aside. All three classes were against me—except Mike. He tried to stand up for me and not let anything bad happen to me, but it wasn't always possible.

Later that day, someone pushed me down the stairs. As I tried to get up, I saw a boy's face from my old class laughing at me and pushing me to the ground again. "You loser," he said as he walked away.

When I was able to stand up, I ran to the bathroom and stayed there for some time. No one could harm me here, and no one would see my crying. I wanted that day to end as soon as possible so I could go home, but I still had two more lessons to go.

During the last lesson, Ava threw water over my math papers. "Oh, I am sorry," she said as she moved away.

I looked at her and then at my papers. Mike tried to clean them and said, "What is your problem, Ava?"

Ava, Liza, and Megan looked at him and said, "None of your business."

I tried to dry them off. As our teacher came, she saw my papers and asked me what had happened. I said that it was my mistake and that I was sorry.

She looked at me and then Mike. Mike shook his head and pointed towards Ava, Liza, and Megan. Our teacher looked at them and got quiet. After class, she called me, Liza, Ava, and Megan to her. We went in front of her.

"Whatever your problem is, you need to solve it because this is unacceptable." Liza replied, "We don't have any problem, but Delilah started it all." I looked at her but kept quiet.

Our teacher had a fierce look towards us and let us go.

When I went out of the classroom, Liza pushed me aside and went downstairs. She went straight to Veronica and Lucy's class, and together they went outside and headed home.

When I entered the garage for my bike, my bike was damaged again. Mike looked at it and said that I couldn't ride it because there was no air in my tires. He walked home with me.

When I reached home, my mum looked at me and said, "What is wrong?" I told her that my bike was damaged again, so I had to walk home. She thought for some time and took me in her arms. After that, I went upstairs and did my homework.

In the afternoon, I went to my granddad to ask him if he could fix my tires again.

I knew that this wasn't the last time they would do this.

I didn't want to go back to school, and I told my parents. They said, "It will be all right. You have to go back to school because you need it. It's not long before until you finish school."

My mum talked to me about what I wanted to do after school and added that I should have a thought about it now, so I could send the paperwork to the companies or schools.

I wanted to try out a musical workshop in my town. There was a chance that they would want me if I was good in dancing, acting, and singing. I needed something to keep my mind busy, apart from all the school drama going on.

Every day at school was just as terrible as I could image it. Everybody teased and laughed at me. One morning I passed the bus station and saw everybody standing there. When they saw me, Max screamed, "Hey you, you little bitch, go die." Then he threw something at me, but I didn't want to look back and see what it was.

I went as fast as possible and tried to ignore it. But after that time, they always waited for me to pass the bus station every morning, and they screamed hurtful words at me.

I was terrified to go to school and pass the bus station alone. Sometimes I tried another way even though it was farther, but for me it was a better way instead of passing them.

My grades went down quickly. Some teachers came to

me and asked what was going on with me, stating that they didn't believe I could get my final done.

When the holidays came for one week, I was relieved. I also had my musical workshop on one of the weekends, so I had something to look forward to, even though I was nervous. During the holidays, I had some singing lessons and got really good at singing. But I still had some difficulties being loud and showing off myself in front of someone else.

My singing teacher also recommended me for one dance school, which was twenty-five minutes away from my home. She said that I should try it out when the holidays were finished.

The weekend arrived when I had my musical workshop for three days. In our first lesson, we introduced ourselves in front of everyone. I was shy about speaking up and telling them who I was, but I took a deep breath and did it. After a while, they said we had to get in pairs so we could do some acting. One girl came straight up to me and asked me if I could work with her. I said yes.

Acting was the one I was most scared of, and my confidence was zero because I had some problems with showing off. We got a small dialogue between two people. They gave us thirty minutes to practice it and came up with our own idea. I was so nervous, and it was very difficult for me to get into the other role.

When the time was up, we had to give our small performance. We were the third group, and the girl and I were very nervous. We did have some problems performing it, but when it was all over, people clapped, and the next group had its turn.

After acting was dancing, where I thought I was good.

But that dance routine was difficult to follow and very fast. I did my best but couldn't keep up with them. I was kind of frustrated because I thought I would do well in dance.

At last we had our singing lessons. We all had to perform one song they gave us with the piano. To everyone's surprise, my singing was the best, and they even wanted me to perform in front of all our families.

The next day, we practiced dance routines from High School Musical and our singing lessons. I didn't have to do a lot of acting and said only one sentence. When they practiced the singing with us, I had problems coming out of my shell. They said I had the best voice, but I didn't come out of myself so that I would make a good performance.

Eventually, two others were chosen to sing on the big day, not me.

After our performance on Sunday, we got our certificates and went home. I wasn't happy about everything because I could have done more, but what was done was done.

After a one-week break from school, we had to go back. I wasn't really happy to go back to school at all. When I stood in front of the school, I just couldn't walk in. I was scared about walking through that door.

My mum gave me a small necklace with a crystal and a cross. She told me I should trust in God and believe he would get me through anything that was coming my way. I held my necklace and took a deep breath. The minute I walked through the door to my classroom, I wanted to run out again.

Everybody had already sat down, and Mike waved at me and gestured that I should come sit with him.

I saw Liza and Ava looking at me and whispering. Meanwhile, Gabriella came to me and asked how I was.

After the small talk, Liza stood up and came towards me. "So now you have to be friends with the losers?" she said with a laugh.

As the bell rang, our teacher came, and we all had to sit down. We had our English class. I was usually pretty good in English, but that term I didn't do anything. It felt like I wasn't worth anything, so I didn't need good grades.

When the big break came, I wanted to go out of my classroom, but Liza, Megan, Lucy, and Veronica stood in my way. I tried to push them aside, but they pushed me back into my classroom and closed the door. It wasn't locked, but they held it tight so I couldn't open it. After some time, they let go and ran away. When I opened the door, I was terrified to go out. I looked everywhere and made sure no one was there to hurt me again.

The minute I walked out, Veronica and Lucy came out of their classroom and pulled on my hair. I froze in place and couldn't move.

"What stupid, dirty hair. Do you even wash it regularly?" they said.

I tried to ignore them and went downstairs into the main hall. As soon as I went into the hall, everybody stared at me and then started laughing. I saw Mike standing outside by the window. He waved at me, but I ran away from everybody.

I ran as fast as I could to a spot behind the sports hall, and I hid for as long as I could. I couldn't stop thinking that maybe it would be easier for me to go. Everybody would have peace and didn't have to talk about me anymore. I wouldn't have to go through this ever again.

After school, I had to walk home again because they damaged my bike like before. Tears ran down my face, and I couldn't hold them back anymore. I simply wanted to go home and be alone.

When I arrived home, my dad told me that my mum was very sick with a very high fever. I knew I couldn't tell her anything about the bullying because she would worry too much. I said hello to her and went straight to my room.

Time passed so slowly. I lay in my bed doing nothing at all. After some time, I went to my Facebook page, and the second I did so, I saw that Veronica posted a picture of my mum from her music band. My mum did look very pretty. In that picture she was younger, so it looked a bit different from now, but she was very beautiful, as she still was today.

Veronica shared the picture and said, "What is with all that stupid make-up? No one from this family can hide her stupid, ugly face."

I scrolled down and saw a picture of me. It said, "And she is the ugliest of all. How could someone even say she has beautiful eyes?" After the comment was a laugh smiley.

I closed Facebook and went to the bathroom. It was all too much, and I couldn't take it anymore. My thoughts were all over the place. I couldn't think straight. I felt alone, scared, and unwanted. As I sat on the floor, I found some small knives in the wardrobe. The minute I saw them, I took one out and thought about what could happen if I ended my life right here, right now. Maybe then everybody would be in peace and wouldn't have to write stupid things about me. Then they could be nice to each other. Maybe I was the one who caused all the problems. Maybe it was me. I was wrong and stupid. I started crying and shaking. I couldn't take it anymore—it was too much.

I held the knife towards my arm. I was about to cut my veins, but suddenly the door opened, and my mum came in. She screamed and took the knife from my hand. She took me in her arms and started crying.

She screamed at me, saying, "Why would you do this? You always need to talk to me about everything. I am here for you."

I told her, "I didn't want to bother anybody anymore and cause problems. I am tired." She looked at me with a sad face and hugged me tight. We sat down on the ground for a long time, just us.

My mum still didn't feel well. I brought her back to her room again so she could lie down. She looked at me and begged me not to do this again, promising that there would always be a solution for the problem. "We will figure it out. I promise," she said.

After that incident, I didn't go back to school for some days. She didn't want to let me out of her sight.

After three days, my mum told me that I should try the dance school my singing teacher had told me about.

I looked it up on the internet and found the address and the timetable. They had a lot of different dance styles in that school. I got excited a little bit. Even though I wasn't sure I really wanted to go there, my mum forced me to go and to have fun again.

The next day, my mum brought me to the dance school. The moment I walked through the door, I felt like I had been here before. The main teacher and boss in this school welcomed me with a hug.

My mum and the teacher talked for some time about what styles I did and which I would like to learn. I had to order some ballet shoes, tights, and suits. The boss's name was Jess, and she was open and friendly to me. She told me that the ballet class would start tomorrow, so I could come back by tomorrow with my usual suit, shoes, and tights.

She hugged me, and we said goodbye.

When I sat down in the car, my mum smiled at me and said, "I think this will be very good for you again."

The next day came, and I eventually had to go back to school. My mum talked to our headmaster and my main teacher about the situation I was in during school. When I arrived at school, I saw Lucy and Veronica standing in front of the bike garage. They stood in front of me and didn't let me out.

"Can I please go?" I begged them.

They laughed and said, "Just so you know, the place is better without you." Then they walked away.

I took a deep breath and walked towards the headmaster's office. He wanted to talk to me that day. My main teacher and my headmaster sat down next to me in the office and asked if it would be possible to have a conversation with Veronica, Lucy, and their parents. I looked at them and told them that I wasn't sure it would change anything, but if necessary I would be there with my mum.

The headmaster nodded and sent me back to my class. I went upstairs to my classroom alone, and everybody was already inside.

When I came inside, I saw Liza, Ava, and Megan looking at me, but they kept quiet.

I sat down and stared at the wall the whole class. Liza came to me after class and said, "Why did you even come back?" Then she went outside laughing with Megan.

I felt so empty, alone, and weak, I wanted to be invisible. During the break, I distanced myself from everyone, but no one cared because nobody wanted anything to do with me. Even the ones who didn't have anything to do with the situation I was in. It was usually just me, Veronica, and Lucy. But everybody made it their problem and stood on their sites, not mine. I simply wanted the school to end now.

When school finished, I went home by myself. My mum talked to me about the conversation we would have with them, and they would tell Lucy and Veronica about it tomorrow. I was scared that this situation would escalate when no one was around, but I had to try.

As I came home, I went to my room and messaged one friend who lived in Portugal. Her name was Sofia, and I met her during our vacations. She was friendly and open towards me. She showed me around the small village and the great beach they had in front of their house.

When I talked to her, I told her everything that was going on and what would happen now. The first thing she said was, "Why don't you try to come here and repeat the last school year?" I thought about it for a moment and liked the idea of it. Of course, it would be difficult because of the language, but I couldn't even stay in my current school the way it was. The only problem would be my headmaster, because he had to give me permission to leave and repeat the year.

After some minutes, I walked downstairs and talked to my parents about it. They weren't too sure about it at first, but eventually they were keen with the idea. "But where are you going to stay? Are you going alone, or do you want one of us to come?" my mum asked me.

I shrugged. "I don't know. But I know I need to get out of here." Unfortunately, I had to pass the conversation with Lucy, Veronica, and their parents first.

I was terrified to go to school the next day because I knew they had asked them about the conversation, and I was scared about how they would react towards me during the day. I couldn't sleep the whole night, and I was awake every hour, imaging about what could happen tomorrow when I went back to school.

After lunch, I had my first lesson of ballet in the new school. I wasn't too happy about it because I would meet new people again and was afraid that they would start talking about me or laughing at me. When I arrived, I went inside and was so nervous that my body started shaking. I saw Jess coming towards me and gave me a big hug. She walked with me to the room and where I could warm up. Everybody was already inside and looking at me. Jess told them about me and added that I wanted to come here every week now. They looked at me and welcomed me. Two girls named Lila and Louise came straight to me. They were so friendly to me and were very generous.

As the class began, we got to the barrier and had a small warm-up and stretch. I loved doing that ballet class, even though it was quiet hard because I hadn't done it in a long time.

After class, Louise came to me and said that if I need

anything or a ride here, I could ask her. Then she gave me her number. I smiled at her and thanked her. When I went out, I saw my mum waiting in the car. She asked me how it went, and I replied, "I loved it. They were so friendly to me, I want to continue coming here and also try to go the hip-hop class." My mum smiled at me and drove home. I was so happy that evening when I came home that I forgot about all the drama that had happened at my old school. After a long and exciting day, I went to bed very tired and felt asleep.

At 7:00 a.m., my alarm rang. I lay in my bed for a few minutes, doing nothing. I held my breath for some time, closed my eyes, and prayed to God that he should be with me on this day and guide me.

When my mum came into my room, she looked at me and saw that I was very worried about today. She gave me a big, long hug.

I needed to get through this without hurting my parents or anybody I loved.

When I arrived at school, everybody was standing in the school hall. I saw Lucy, Veronica, Amelia, Sophia, and Liza standing in front of the stairs, talking. As I walked past them, Lucy held me back and pushed me on my shoulder. "What the hell do you think you are doing? Acting like we are the bad ones? Are you stupid? You will see what you have done now."

I walked upstairs as fast as I could and sat on my desk. My head felt so heavy, and my thoughts were so many. I was so scared to look back or behind me. I wanted it to be over right now.

After school, I went to get my bike as usual, but before I was able to get it, Lucy and Veronica stood blocking it. I tried to ignore them and get to my bike, but they pushed me down to the ground.

Lucy looked down at me and said, "You'll wish you had never said anything to anyone, believe me." Then they walked away. I froze again and couldn't move.

After several minutes, I was able to get up and ride home. I wanted to cry so hard but held it together for my parents. When I reached home, I rushed upstairs and lay in my bed for the whole day.

My mum came inside after a few hours and asked about my day. I didn't respond, and she just closed the door knowing it wasn't good.

The next day, we had our conversation. I was nervous as hell. I couldn't breathe, sleep, or eat at all that day. The minute I reached school with my mum, I saw Veronica and her mum standing in front of the headmaster's office. Veronica's mum looked at us very disappointed. I couldn't think why she would be disappointed in us—it was her daughter who had bullied me for years.

After a few minutes, Lucy's mother arrived but without Lucy. In that moment, I knew that Lucy knew exactly what she had done to me else, or else she would have shown up. She was a coward.

When our teacher and the headmaster came out, we followed them into a room. We sat down on each side, and then it started. Our teacher looked at Lucy's mum and asked where Lucy was.

"She didn't feel so well, and I thought that this wouldn't be a big deal, because she didn't do anything wrong," her mother said.

Our teacher looked at me depressed. The headmaster

asked everyone if they knew why we were called here this meeting.

Veronica and her mother said that they were not sure about all this. Her mother looked at us and added, "My daughter would never hurt anybody. How can you assume she is doing that to her?"

My mum wanted to speak up, but I told her to keep quiet for now. Our headmaster asked Lucy's mother about everything—if Lucy had bullied me these past few years. She simply said, "She is so innocent, she couldn't hurt anybody. She is exactly like Veronica. She would never do this. Maybe it is Delilah, and she is trying to hide it now, behind others."

What did she just say?

Veronica looked at me, and I just couldn't believe that they were all lying in front of me. My teacher and the headmaster knew exactly what was going on in school, and they still lied. I kept quiet the whole time and listened. I wasn't sure what to say because the mothers believed that their children were so innocent and couldn't hurt a fly. I was overwhelmed with the situation.

The headmaster tried to explain that I had been off school for some time, because people bullied me aggressively every day in school. He added that they had seen some incidents during school time with their daughters and me.

The mothers shook their heads and repeatedly said that their daughters would never do this to me. They still thought that we were all good friends, or at least that was what they said.

But deep down I knew they knew everything. Maybe it wasn't wrong to stand next to your daughter because that was what every mother should do, but in that kind of situation, where someone got bullied every day and wanted to kill herself, the parents should be teaching their daughters a lesson, not giving them a blessing.

After forty-five minutes of talking, it was finally over. Lucy's mother rushed out of the room and headed straight home.

Veronica and her mother came to me and said, "I am so sad that you didn't talk to me first, before all his. Maybe we could have solved it."

My mum and I walked out and went quietly to our car. Yes, maybe we could have come earlier to Veronica and her mother to talk. But would it really have worked? I didn't believe so.

When we reached home, we sat down with my dad and talked about what would happen now. We told him how the conversation was and added that everybody said they didn't do anything wrong.

My looked at us and said, "Let's go to bed, have sleep, and talk tomorrow." I went straight to bed but couldn't sleep because I knew I had to face them in school again. And what would happen now? I didn't want to think about it, but I couldn't help myself. I was terrified to go back to school.

The next morning, my mum came to me and said, "Why don't you ask your headmaster about Portugal? Maybe there will be a chance you can go there for a few months and then repeat the last class." I was speechless, but she was right. I went as usual to school, but before I went to my classroom, I summoned up my courage and when to the office of my headmaster. I was nervous but knew I needed to do something.

I knocked on the door, and he let me in. He looked at me sadly and said, "Well, that should have been better yesterday. I am sorry."

I nodded and spoke up. "If am allowed, I would like to ask you something." He nodded, and I continued. "I know this is short notice, but as far as I see it, I won't be able to make the last year and our final exam. I have bad grades and can't concentrate on anything during class. So I guess I need to repeat the last year anyway. I wanted to ask you if it's possible for me to leave to Portugal go to school there for a few months and come back to repeat the last school year. I know this is a lot, but I am terrified every morning to come to school."

He looked at me surprised and said, "I will think about it and let you know."

When I went outside, I was relieved I had asked him, and I prayed that he would say yes.

The minute I went upstairs, I saw Lucy and Veronica standing in front of the classroom. Lucy looked at me and said, "I am sorry I couldn't be there yesterday, but I wasn't feeling well. And you know I never hurt you. Everybody knows." She gave a fake cough.

I walked inside my classroom and sat down. My chair made a noise, but it didn't bother me. Then I saw Lucy standing inside my classroom, yelling, "Delilah is so fat, she can't even sit down on her chair without it falling apart."

All of a sudden, our headmaster walked in and took Lucy by her arm. He angrily said, "This is not your classroom. Go to your seat and sit down immediately."

He looked at me, saw my tears running down my face,

and nodded. He closed the door behind him, and I tried to continue breathing.

I thought to myself, You have to keep breathing. Inhale and exhale.

During the break and even until the school was finish, I didn't see or hear anything from Veronica or Lucy again. It was like they had vanished from the place.

After school, my teacher said that I should come with her to the headmaster's office. I walked with her and waited until we could go inside. When he opened the door, he let us in, and I sat down quietly. He looked at me and said, "I have seen this for months, what they have done to you. I always believed it would get better, but it didn't, and it will not get better for you. I release you from the rest of the school year. You can go to Portugal for a few months and come back to repeat the last year."

I smiled at him and wanted to cry, but not because I was sad—I was so happy. He added that I didn't have to come back to school. I should come tomorrow to pack all my stuff from my locker. Then I should plan my trip to Portugal and search for a school because he still wanted to have some paper that said that I was attending school. I thanked him, ran to my bike, and rushed home.

When I reached home, I ran to my mum and told her that I was allowed to go. She looked at me and hugged me tight. It was one of my happiest moments. I couldn't believe this was really happening. I couldn't hold back my tears and let everything out. That moment was a relief, and my body finally could rest from all the stress that had happened. I whispered, "Thank you, God."

CHAPTER 6

NEW START

Finally, after three weeks off school, with no friends and no phone, I had the chance to go to Portugal and attend a school. My friend Sofia was very happy when she heard I was coming.

The day before I was going to leave, I went to Nicola's house for the last time. I would stay there for about three months until my school was finished. She wasn't happy about it, but she could understand it perfectly.

We ate some pizza, watched some movies together, and had a good laugh. I enjoyed every moment with her and thanked her for being there for me during this time.

After all this time, I was allowed to use my Facebook page again. I logged in and immediately wished I hadn't. I had many messages and comments on my pictures. My heart beat so fast, and my hands started shaking. After a deep breath, I had the courage to open some messages. Almost all of them were from Lucy, Veronica, or Liza. Veronica and Lucy wrote in one message that I was a coward who ran away from nothing. They hoped that I was dead so they didn't have to see my face again.

The other message was from Liza, and it said, "So you are just leaving without saying goodbye to your friends?"

Another message came from Lucy. "How stupid are you to run away? You think we can't catch you anywhere else? Be ready for the worst. We will catch you during the night and day."

After that, I couldn't read any more messages. I was so terrified about what would be written. I closed my computer and packed my things. I took some nice shoes, dresses and skirts, and my new bikini I had bought. I was ready to leave and have a clean break without stressing out.

My mum told me that she had found an apartment online, near the school. The owner would pick us up from the airport and bring us to the place. She was so relieved that she had found a place for us to stay. We also knew that we couldn't afford staying there together for months. Eventually we had to find a host family where I would stay—alone.

I couldn't really fall asleep that night. I was very nervous about meeting new people, living in a new place, and managing the new surroundings.

The next morning, our flight was very early. I said goodbye to my grandparents and my brother. My dad drove us to the airport. During the ride, I thought about everything that had happened these last months. A tear rolled down my face, and I prayed to God, "Please, this time let me have some good friends and some good times with them."

When we reached the airport, my dad followed us to the check-in, and after we left our baggage at the gate, we said goodbye to each other with a tight hug. He wished me the best and hoped to see me and my mum very soon. After the goodbye, we went into the security lounge. We had a last wave goodbye and went into the airport shops.

Finally it was time to go in the airplane. I was nervous but excited at the same time. It was a big, brave step, as my mum always said. For me, it was time to leave my old school and have some time without all the fake friends, rumors, and bullying. When we sat down in the plane, my mum looked at me and said, "I am so happy we are able to do this." I looked at her and smiled. It was a long trip, and I listened to music most of the time and relaxed. We had to transfer once and then finally we were on the plane to Portugal.

After a two-hour flight, we finally landed on time in Portugal. It was hot but amazing. The moment we went out of the airplane, we saw the man who was to pick us up. He had a sign with our name on. We smiled at him and went forward. He spoke English pretty well because he taught in an international school. He had also lived in Holland for quite some time.

"I hope your flight was well and that you are ready to have some great heat here," he said with a smile. My mum talked with him the entire ride to the apartment. He was friendly and open to us, and he told us that they also had a pool inside the area. If we needed to rent a car, we should ask him where the place was, and he would show us.

About thirty-five minutes later, we reached the place. It was on the beach, and I loved it. It was so beautiful and open to the ocean. He helped us bring our bags upstairs and told us everything we needed to know about the place. After some talking, he gave us the number for his wife as well and said we could always call her if anything was wrong. We thanked him, and he left.

We thought about renting a car the next day so we would be able to buy some essentials. My mum and I went outside to the beach. It was like a dream come true. I could finally breathe again. I was free.

We sat down for a while, stared at the ocean, and didn't do anything. After almost an hour, we went upstairs to our apartment. The man had left us some essentials for the evening, so we had something small to eat. We went to bed after a small shower. I was so tired from the trip and quickly fell asleep.

It was the weekend, so I didn't need to go to school straight away. The next morning, we went out to rent a car. We found it straight away and got a really nice but small car. After we rented it, we went to the supermarket to buy food and drinks. It was difficult to find a store, but we eventually found a big one where we were able to buy everything. There was even a big shopping mall not far from our place.

We didn't speak or understand any Portuguese, but we tried and gestured with hands. The people in Portugal didn't speak English well, but some at least tried to. When we finished our shopping, we drove around to the beach, and we wanted to see how far it was to the school.

As we passed the school, my hurt stopped for a second. I couldn't believe I would really go to this school, where I couldn't even speak the language. And I didn't have anybody except Sofia. But Sofia didn't even go to this school. She went to the school next door, so I wouldn't see or meet her during school time. However, I stayed in contact with Sofia and would meet her many times.

I felt so nervous but knew I had to do it. I had come this far for something, and I didn't want to go back to my old school. I had to go here and at least try my best. After some relaxing days, we went out to eat in the shopping mall. The food was nice, and I enjoyed every second. My mum and I went around the mall after we ate. We saw many nice dresses and shoes. And the clothes were even my size, because most of the people here were as short as I was.

I had a good chance to get new clothes and especially jeans here. When we reached home, my mum called my dad, and they talked for some time. I went to the beach alone, just me and my thoughts. I didn't want to think back again, but I couldn't stop thinking about all that had happened to me. I just hoped that it wouldn't happen here in a few months. While I sat on the beach, I took my phone out and went to Facebook again. I saw some pictures from Veronica and Lucy enjoying themselves at a party and smoking. My first thought was that I was happy not be a part of them anymore because of all the smoking and drugs they were doing. But I was also jealous that they had the kind of friendship I had missed for a long time.

Later, I went upstairs to my mum, and we sat on the balcony and talked about a lot of things because the next day, I had to go for my first day of school. She told me that I had to meet the headmaster before I went to class, and she would bring me to my new class.

That evening I went to bed early to have a good night's sleep for the coming day.

The next morning arrived far too quickly, and I had to get ready for my first day in the new school. When I drove with my mum to the school, I was so nervous that my voice shook. I couldn't hold it back, but I was ready and wanted to move forward.

When we arrived, everybody went inside the school. Because I was blonde, everybody looked at me. Not a lot of people were blonde in Portugal, at least not naturally blonde. I was the only blonde girl in that crowd outside. My mum and I went inside the school hall and searched for the headmaster's office. When we reached it, we knocked at the door and went straight in.

"Welcome. I am so happy to finally meet you. Everybody is waiting for you," the headmaster said to me.

I looked at my mum, and she nodded and walked to our car.

"Come with me. I will bring you to your new classroom and introduce you to everyone. They already know you are coming, and a lot of pupils here can speak English, so they will help you through the lessons," she said.

We walked along the halls, and she told me where the cafeteria was and added that I could always get food here for the breaks, though I had to pay for it. When we reached the classroom, my heart dropped, and I held my breath for a minute. The headmaster and I walked inside the classroom, where the students were already in their seats.

"Hello, class, this is Delilah, your new student for three months." Everybody stood up and welcomed me.

The teacher came towards me and gestured to where I should sit. I was sitting next to a girl named Carolina. The teacher told me, "She speaks fluent English, so you will understand each other."

I nodded and sat down.

"Hey, I am Carolina. I am so happy to finally meet you," Carolina said to me with a smile.

I sat down and tried to understand what they were talking about, because it was the Portuguese class. Carolina gave me a paper and tried to explain everything that they talked about. She tried to translate it on the paper from Portuguese to English.

We laughed and had some fun writing and learning the language. They all tried to teach me how to understand and speak Portuguese, but it wasn't easy at all. This language was difficult for me.

All the pupils in my class were open and friendly to me every day. They walked home with me, or we went to eat together after school and sometimes during the evenings as well. We became close quite quickly. It was a great feeling to be with them.

One day, Carolina invited me over to her place to have some dinner. I was so delighted and said yes. That evening I went to her apartment. She was living with her mum and her dog. It was a lovely apartment, and I liked it. We had a lovely small dinner together, I tried to talk in Portuguese, and we spoke in English too. I loved the food her mum made for us; it was very Portuguese but was so delicious. Her mum was friendly to me.

Then there was Clara and Ana, who always came to me and talked to me every day. Ana loved doing music and dancing. She danced ballet and played the piano. Clara was very talented too. She played the piano and sang. She had a very beautiful voice and was very special. Sometimes I went to her house, and we played piano together and sang a song. Ana asked me one day in school if I would like to join her ballet class sometime. I immediately said yes, because I think I gained weight during the time here due to not doing much for sports. I also enjoyed the new food everywhere.

One evening I went on the train to Ana's place, and we went together to the ballet studio. In Portugal, they practiced for competitions, and one needed to be really good, or else they would never take the person to higher levels. They pushed the pupils to limit, and sometimes one could see how tired they were. Some were also very arrogant.

I loved the ballet lesson, and Ana was very good. However, she couldn't focus on it as much as she would love to, she told me, because of school and good grades and the final exams that would come this year.

Every day it was like a new adventure in school. I never knew what would happen. I still tried to learn the language, but it was difficult. Everybody helped me through classes and enjoyed my company.

I loved being in school again. Students involved me in every activity they were doing at school and even after school.

I had the courage to go into my Facebook account, and I deleted Veronica, Lucy, Liza, and all the others. The moment I did that, I felt free. I knew they were still able to write me if they wanted to, but at least they couldn't see what I was posting or doing.

After about one month, my mum told me that we needed to find a host family for me because we couldn't afford to stay any longer in the apartment. We prayed that to God that he would send us a sign, because we couldn't think of anyone who was doing this.

When I went to school the next day, I asked Rafaela if

it was possible to stay with her for two months. She looked at me and smiled. "I will ask my mother and let you know."

After school, I got a text message from Carolina saying, "I am sorry, but my mum didn't allow it, because we will have some visitors over in a few weeks."

I replied, "OK, don't worry. I will find something."

During the day, my mum went into a cafe near my school. She drank a coffee and ate some cake. She heard a woman speaking English to her daughter, and my mum immediately smiled at her. The woman sat at the opposite table from my mum. Her daughter smiled at my mother the whole time. My mum started talking and said, "You look so beautiful with your lovely hair."

The woman looked at my mum and asked, "So you are not from here? We just moved here too."

My mum introduced herself and told her about me going to school and trying to find a host family for me. They talked all afternoon about a lot of things. After some time, they had to go, but the woman said, "If you still need a host family after a week, let me know. I would love to do that." Then she and her daughter went outside and drove home.

My mum picked me up from school. She smiled at me and said, "I think I found a host family for you. You have to meet her first, but she seems really nice and has a daughter." I was very happy to hear that. We immediately set a lunch date for the next day. I hoped and prayed that it would work out in a positive way for me.

CHAPTER 7

BRAVE

The next day arrived, and we met the woman with her daughter in our favourite restaurant on the beach. When she arrived, she greeted us, and we sat down. We ordered some pizza for everybody and drank our drinks.

"So you are Delilah, and you really want to stay here without your mother for two more months?" the woman said.

I replied, "Yes, I would love to."

We smiled at each other and had a nice, long conversation. She explained that she had a small apartment on the fourth floor. But she had one guest room, if I wanted to stay with her.

My mum asked about how we would do everything, like buying food or anything else I would need. They set up an agreement, and everybody was happy with it. "I would like to show you our place, if you liked to see it before you decide," the woman said.

After lunch, we went down the street towards her apartment. Under her apartment was a pharmacy and a small shop where I could get some bread and magazines. We went upstairs, and I carefully looked around her apartment.

It was small, but I liked it, and her daughter was very keen with me. After some time, I played with the daughter a little, and we had some tea and coffee. When we all finished, my mum and I said goodbye to them and added that we would be in contact within the coming days. We went to our car and drove back to our place.

"I think this will be a good host family for me," I said. My mum agreed. But she also told me if anything was wrong and I didn't like it anymore, I should call her. She would come as soon as possible and take me back. When we reached home, I sat on the balcony and thought a lot about whether I would be brave enough to be alone here with a woman I didn't know for a long time.

The next day, I went to school as usual and talked to my friends about it. They were happy that I had found somewhere to stay. They said that I should definitely do it, and even if something went wrong, they would be here for me. I was happy that they told me this because I knew I wasn't alone here, even when my mum would not be here for me.

The school day went as usual, and I even understood some words in Portuguese after one month. Sometimes I also tried to speak to my friends, but they didn't always understand me. But hey, at least I tried.

After school, I went to eat with Carolina and the others in a small restaurant next to our school and near the beach. I think I loved the food too much there, because I gained weight, but at least I felt confident in my body. I dressed nicely every day and tried to wear more dresses and skirts. I even got a bit tan, because it was always sunny during the day. Also, sometimes we went to the beach after school, lay down on the sand, and had a nice long tan day. We went into the ocean sometimes, but I was scared because the waves were enormous sometimes, so I preferred to stay on land.

Time went by so fast that the day came when my mother had to leave. I was very sad but was sure I could do this without her. She brought me to the woman who would take care of me, and before she left, she looked at me and said, "If anything is wrong, call me, and I will come back." I nodded and gave her a big hug. When she went into her car and drove away, a little tear fell down my face, but I knew it would be all right.

After some time, I went inside the new apartment. The woman had dinner ready for me and her daughter. When I sat down, I saw that the little daughter was under the table and eating her food. It was very lovely with me and the woman. We talked about school, my hobbies, and my family. She also told me a lot about herself and admitted that she liked golfing on weekend with her daughter, so I could join them. She showed me to my room and gave me some space but said that this room had been full before she had taken all the things out. She therefore wanted me to sleep in the small basement. I was kind of shocked when she said that to me. How could she even suggest that I sleep in a basement? The door closed behind her, and I lay on my bed for a minute breathing in and out. I had to realize that this was really happening.

When I lay on my bed, I went on my phone and to my Facebook account. At that moment I got a message from Lucy.

"How are you, fat face? We do not miss you here, and I hope you will not come back," she wrote.

I deleted the message and tried to forget it. I didn't want her to come near me again with her hurtful messages. After I unpacked my stuff and put them in the wardrobe, I went to the living room to join the daughter for some TV.

Her name was Lilly, and the woman's name was Ingrid. We had a lovely evening together, and I enjoyed their company.

The first night was really hard for me because I had never been that far away from my parents. I couldn't sleep all night, I turned from side to side, and sometimes I heard weird noises coming from outside.

I tried not to panic but felt terrified to even go to the bathroom. My blanket was all over me, and I tried to ignore the noises so that I would finally fall asleep.

After a long and stressful night, my alarm rang, and I had to get ready for school.

I was so tired that I couldn't walk properly. I made some breakfast for myself, and because Ingrid and Lilly were still sleeping, I tried to be very quiet. I made some cereal and took some water out of the fridge. I sat down and saw how the sun rose high. It was a lovely view, and I loved waking up like this. It had a relaxing touch when one had a rough night.

When it was 7:30, I had to rush to school because I was almost too late. I got there just in time. Carolina and Ana were already waiting for me in front of the school hall. They hugged me tight when they saw me.

"How are you feeling, and how was your first night in the new apartment?" Carolina asked.

"It was a very rough night, but I hope it will be better in time," I said. They nodded, and we went to our classroom.

As soon as I sat in class, my eyes started to close. I was so tired from the night before and couldn't hold myself up anymore. I had to get through this day so I could go home and head straight to bed.

After school, my friends asked me if I wanted to come to dinner with them. I was simply too tired to do anything, so I said no and went home.

When I came home, no one was there, so I was alone and tired. I wanted to go to my bed and sleep. My phone rang after I lay in my bed. It was my mum. I immediately picked up and was so happy to hear her voice. "Hello, my love. How are you?" she asked me.

"I am very tired because I didn't sleep last night, but otherwise I am all right," I responded. She asked me about my day and how everything went in the morning. I said that everything was going well so far, and I didn't have anything to complain about. After a few minutes, I told her that I wanted to rest, so we closed our call and promised to talk later in the evening.

My eyes were so heavy that they closed. It was very light from the sun outside, so my room was full of sunlight. However, I was able to fall asleep very quickly because I didn't have to worry about any noises or creatures.

After an hour, I heard the door opening. "Hey there. Just wanted to let you know that we are home, and I am making dinner now," Ingrid said, and then she closed the door.

I rubbed my face and stood up. When I went outside my room, Lilly came to me and gave me a big hug.

"How are you, little girl?" I asked her. She smiled and ran to the TV.

I went to the kitchen and saw Ingrid cooking dinner. She looked at me and smiled. "How was your day today?"

"It was not bad, but I was very tired, so I lay down for an hour," I said. She nodded and continued with the food preparation. I asked her if she needed help, but she shook her head and said that I should sit down with her daughter.

We sat down and watched some TV. She watched Hannah Montana, and I liked the show as well, so I enjoyed watching with her.

After thirty minutes, the food was ready, and we set the table. We put the food down, and I gave a small prayer in my mind.

When we finished eating, I helped Ingrid clean, and after we finished, I went to take a long shower.

The minute I came out of the bathroom, it was almost time for me to go to bed, but I wanted to call my mum before I went to sleep. I called her and my dad. We had a nice, short chat, and after a while I hung up the phone and went to bed.

It was dark again, and I had the feeling that something or someone was in my room—some dark energy. I couldn't see anything but felt it deep in my bones. Every time I lay with my face to the wall, I was terrified to turn around. My heart started beating very fast. I prayed to God that he should continue protecting me, and I thanked him for everything he had done for me in the past few months. After the prayer, I tried to put on some music, close my eyes, and sleep. It worked quite well for me, so the next morning I had a nice deep sleep until my alarm rang again.

When the sun rose, I woke up, dressed myself, and made some breakfast for myself. After some time, I left the apartment and went straight to school to meet Carolina and Ana in front of the school.

During my walk to the school, I couldn't stop thinking about how something was following me in the apartment. It felt like I wasn't alone, even when I couldn't see it, but I felt it during the night. It was very strange, but I couldn't let this ruin my stay with the woman, so I didn't say anything to anyone and kept it to myself.

This feeling was there every single night, and sometimes it was worse. I remembered one night in my hometown when I woke up during the night, and some black creature was standing next to my bed and looking at me. The second I thought about that, I got goosebumps all over my body. I didn't want to see all these souls, dark energies, or whatever, but I knew something was in that apartment.

The days passed quickly, and I talked to my mum every day. I wanted to hear her voice, and I wished that she would be here with me most of the time.

"You are so brave," my brother sometimes said to me. I couldn't really see it as brave—I didn't have any other choice.

One weekend we went to golf near the beach. I had never golfed before, but it was a lot of fun. After that session, we went to eat some pizza outside. When we had dinner, we usually ate noodles with some tomato sauce. Ingrid said that her daughter didn't eat anything else, so she always made the same food.

I had to accept it, but I always thought it was strange. At least let the child try some new food. Maybe she would be surprised that she actually liked other foods. When we went into that restaurant and ordered some pizza, they shared a very small pizza together, and both of them ate just one piece and took the rest home. I felt so fat that I ate almost all of a pizza by myself. I also wondered why they ate that little every time we went out for dinner, or even in the house. Every time I asked Lilly if she wanted to try a piece of my food, Ingrid always said, "No, she wouldn't want that." Eventually we walked home and talked about a lot of different things. Ingrid told me that she had to go Braga, to leave her daughter at her dad's house for the two days. She asked me if I wanted to come along. I said of course. She told me that she wasn't too keen with Lilly's dad anymore, so I should stay in the car when we arrived. He dealt with drugs and all other things. I nodded, and we walked straight up to the apartment. When she told me about Lilly's father, I wondered whether he was so bad as she had told me. If so, why would she give her daughter to him for two days? If he really was a drug dealer, I wouldn't let my daughter near him. It was very strange.

When we reached home, it was very late, and I went to my room to have some alone time. I wrote messages with my mum and told her everything that was going on. I mentioned that I would go to Braga with Ingrid the next weekend. When I had to sleep, I couldn't stop thinking about all of this. Something weird was about Ingrid and her daughter, but I couldn't figure out what it was. That night it was very quiet, and I hated it. I liked it when there were some cars driving outside or people speaking. I put on my music and closed my eyes.

During the night, I suddenly woke up and couldn't move. I saw a small shadow passing my window. That time I wasn't sure whether I was dreaming or whether it was real. I tried to move but couldn't; it was like I was paralyzed.

After some time, I could move, and I turned on the light. It was almost morning, so I was lucky. I waited until the sun rose a bit and turned off my light. My heart was heavy, and I was so terrified when I woke up that my body was wet all over. I took a quick shower before school and went to school afterwards without breakfast. I simply wanted to get out of the apartment.

During my walk to school, I stopped at a cafe and bought a croissant to eat. On my way to school, I met Clara, and we walked together the rest of the way. "You look so tired. What happened?" she asked me. "Nothing. I just didn't sleep well again last night," I said.

She said that if anything was bothering me, I could talk to her. I nodded, and we moved along.

The school day was usual. I tried my best with everything, but it didn't get easier anytime soon.

After school, we all went out for some beach time. We packed our bikinis, went straight to the beach, and lay in the sun.

"So, what do you think about Portugal now?" Carolina asked me.

"I love it. There is nothing more to say." I smiled at her.

Everybody grinned, and we went into the ocean, but just a little because it was very cold. The ocean was calm, with no big waves. It was so relaxing to hear the sound of the ocean.

I looked at the ocean and thought, Yes, I am brave, confident, and beautiful. And I was able to come here and stay by myself. I did this—no one else. I closed my eyes, felt the wind in my face, and enjoyed the sounds of everything was around me. I had positive energy and positive thoughts.

CHAPTER 8

CONFUSING

After our long beach day, I went straight home for dinner. When I reached home, Ingrid stood at the door and said, "Where were you the whole time after school finished? I needed some help."

I was confused and said that I had told her I was going to the beach with my friends.

She glared at me and walked away. I shook my head and went into my room to change. After a few minutes, I went to the table to eat. Lilly sat under the table again, and I asked her if she wanted to sit with us. Her mum waved her hand at me as if to say, Don't ask her. I looked down at my food and couldn't stop thinking about what was happening right now.

Something was odd with her, more than before. Yes, she was weird from the first day, but today she was strange towards me.

The minutes passed, and finally Ingrid started talking to me and asking about my day instead of yelling at me.

"I had a great day with my friends, and especially with Carolina. She is really kind to me," I said.

She replied, "Well, that doesn't last long. Just until she finds a better friend than you."

I couldn't say anything to that because she knew what I had gone through in my hometown. To have said that was rude. I ignored it and smiled slightly.

After dinner, Lilly told me that she had her first ballet class tomorrow and was excited about it.

"Do you want me to bring you tomorrow so your mum has some free time?" I asked Lilly, but I looked at her mum.

"Oh, no, no, don't ask that again. I will do it," she said, almost yelling at me.

I nodded, took my plate to the kitchen, and washed it.

"Let me wash. You just go and relax," Ingrid said.

I gave her my plate and went into my room. I didn't have enough money on my phone, so I called my mum with the house telephone, which Ingrid allowed me to use. I talked to her about half an hour, discussing school and how everyone was at home. After some time, I said goodbye and went to the living room. "I am going to bed now, so I just wanted to say good night," I said to them.

Ingrid looked at me and nodded.

I went into my room, changed into my pyjamas, and lay on my bed to listen to some music. I went to my Facebook page and saw that Carolina had posted some pictures of our group from the beach. They were so great, and I had a big smile on my face. I couldn't stop smiling because I was finally happy again and felt like myself in front of my friends.

When I was about to turn off my light, I heard some strange noise in front of my door. I opened it slightly and saw a shadow running away.

First I thought maybe it was Lilly, but I knew she was already in bed. It could have been Ingrid, but why would she do this? To see if I was already asleep, or spying on what I was doing? I didn't want to think any further about it, so I tried to sleep.

During the night, I woke up again because of a noise. It sounded like someone had just closed my door. My heart beat so fast, and I felt sweat coming down my back. I couldn't go look because I was too scared, so I tried to close my eyes and sleep.

The next morning, I decided that because I had a day off school, I would meet my friends at the beach again and have some lunch with them. Especially because Ingrid didn't want me to help her with anything.

I told Ingrid about my plans. She nodded at me and said, "I hope you enjoy yourself here, while you can." I turned away and walked out the door. What was going on with her? Why was she so rude to me? Had I done something wrong? I always tried to help her out.

When I reached the beach, the sun was very hot. I saw Carolina and Ana already waiting for me. We searched a place for us to put our towels, and we lay down and ate some fruits. The ocean looked so lovely today, the wind was calm, and the waves were quiet.

When we lay down, I told Carolina about last night. "Do you think it was the woman?" she asked me.

Ana said, "Maybe it wasn't really closed, and she just wanted to close it fully." I didn't know what to say because I wasn't sure what had really happened. After some sunbathing, we went to eat at a nearby restaurant and met some other friends from school. We sat together and had fun the whole time. When we finished, Carolina brought me to the apartment. During this walk, we talked about nothing special. As I reached the apartment, I looked up and didn't want to go inside, but I knew I had to.

"You know, if anything is wrong, let me know," Carolina said to me, and she hugged me tight.

I went upstairs, opened the door, and saw Ingrid and Lilly sitting in the living room. When I went inside and said hello, they didn't really look at me and just nodded. I raised my eyebrows and shook my head. After that, I took a quick shower and went into my room. I wanted to lay down on my bed, but my door opened without a knock.

"I hope you had a great day with your friends. We will go to Braga tomorrow.

Do you still want to come, or do you prefer to stay with your great friends?" she asked me, looking quite jealous.

"Yes, I will go with you," I said.

She nodded and said good night. I lay down on my bed and couldn't fall asleep easily because Ingrid was not acting normal. It seemed like she was jealous because I had friends who liked me and appreciated me. But she was older than me, so why should she be jealous of me?

After a sleepless night again, I awoke and went to have breakfast with them. When I came into the kitchen, she looked up from the table and said, "You are late. We want to leave in thirty minutes, so be ready." I nodded, ate some cereal, and got myself ready.

After thirty minutes, we went downstairs to her car and started our two-hour drive to Braga with her daughter. That drive was one of the worst rides I had ever had. She didn't put on music often, and when it was, it was classical.

When I asked her if I could get a small snack, she almost

shouted at me. "Not in my car! You have to wait until we are there."

I immediately put my snack back in my bag and looked out the window. Every time I wanted to start a conversation with her, she ignored it or simply nodded and continued driving. After almost an hour, Lilly's teddy fell down. I wanted to reach it and give it to her, but Ingrid took my arm away and shook her head. "If she lets it fall, she has to deal with it herself," she said, angry.

"I don't have any problem giving it to her. It's not far from me, and I am able to reach it," I replied.

She stared at me and said no. I looked at Lilly and how sad she was. I couldn't believe why Ingrid was acting like this in front of her daughter.

Finally, after two hours, we reached the house of Lilly's dad. She jumped out and ran into his arms. Lilly looked very happy to see him and immediately showed him her new teddy bear. He waved at me and went inside with Ingrid and her daughter. I wasn't allowed to get out of the car, so I looked out of the window.

I wondered about the dad. If he was really dealing with drugs or had done it in the past, why did he had a nice house like this? He looked normal to me. Yes, maybe he had gone through something, but now he looked like a normal human being.

When Ingrid came out, I could see anger in her face. She closed the car door and started driving back.

"We will have to pick her up tomorrow morning. You don't need to come. I know you like to sleep long on weekends, so don't bother waking up." I didn't want to say anything because I could see that maybe something happened inside, and it made her very angry. I ignored her during the silent trip back and focused on the outside.

When we finally arrived, it was already evening, and we had to get dinner ready. As we went upstairs, she looked at me and said, "I don't have any food at home, so if you want to eat something warm, you need to go out and eat. I am going to my room, so don't bother me, and don't be too loud."

I nodded and was very confused at how she was reacting, like I had harmed her or done something wrong to her. I was never loud when they were asleep. I was always careful when I did something in the kitchen or living room. As such, I didn't know what upset her so much.

Eventually I went outside and met Carolina. I had texted her on the way back home. She met me at our favourite restaurant near the beach.

"So now you don't even get food at home?" she laughed and shook her head. I shook my head too and started to eat. We talked about Ingrid the whole evening. None of us understood why she would act like this towards me. I was even afraid to go back home and sleep there.

Carolina told me that I could come to her place for tonight and have a sleepover. I hugged her but said that I needed to go back, or else Ingrid would find another reason to be angry at me. After we finished the food, we went our separate ways. I stood in front of the apartment and didn't hear anything inside; it was very quiet and kind of scary.

When I opened the door and closed it, I went straight into my room and turned on my light. That night I didn't see or hear anything from Ingrid. I called my mum and told her that something wasn't right, and I didn't feel safe here anymore. The way Ingrid was acting in front of me wasn't OK—it was mean. My mum understood and asked if she should come and get me.

"No, let's wait a bit and see," I said. She agreed, and we said goodbye. I went straight to sleep with my headphones in my ears.

As the sun rose, I awoke quickly and heard a lot of noises coming from the kitchen. I stood up and went into the kitchen. "Good morning."

Ingrid looked and said, "Oh, so you're up early today." She continued making her breakfast to take on her drive. "I am going now, so you have to manage alone today for your food." Then she went out the door.

When she closed the door, I immediately called my parents from the house telephone to hear their voices. After some time, I made some breakfast; as always, I had cereal because there was nothing more in the fridge. I ate and texted Carolina and Ana to meet up after breakfast. They both replied, "Let's meet on the beach."

After I finished my breakfast, I cleaned my plate, packed my things, and went to the beach. It was a very nice and sunny day. This day was very relaxing with no stress or anger. We lay on the beach for a few hours, played volleyball, and ate the snacks Carolina's mum had made for us.

After lunch, I went back home and got into the shower. When I came out of the shower, I heard footsteps towards the bathroom. I had locked the door, so no one could come in.

"It's me, Ingrid. Just wanted to let you know we are back," she said. My heart dropped because for a second, I had panicked thinking it was an intruder. When I came out of the bathroom, I went into the living room. Lilly sat on the floor playing with her new toys. "Yes, he bought her something new—again," Ingrid said.

I looked at Lilly and saw how happy she was about her new toy. I sat down next to her.

"Did you already eat lunch?" Ingrid asked me.

"Yes, I did, with Carolina," I replied.

She rolled her eyes. "OK, great."

After I played a bit with Lilly, Ingrid came and took Lilly to her room. I was very confused. "She needs some quiet time now. Go do something else, but nothing with her," Ingrid said to me. She closed the door to Lilly's room.

I shook my head, sat down on the floor for a minute, and thought about why she had done that. Was she jealous of me being good with her daughter? What was the problem here?

After some minutes, I went into my room and called my mum again. I told her that something happened again, and it made me feel like I wasn't welcome here anymore. When we finished our phone call, I went straight to bed without any dinner. Ingrid didn't ask if I wanted to eat something. I closed my eyes, and because it was still a bit sunny outside, I fell asleep quickly and slept through the night.

When I woke up the next morning, I had an early call from my mum. "I am coming to get you and take you to a place where we both can stay," she said. "Why? I didn't say you should come," I replied.

"Ingrid called me yesterday and said that I have to come get you, because this isn't working anymore, and she doesn't want you in her apartment. You are not helping her in the house or with her daughter."

I couldn't speak for some time and started to cry. I

hadn't done anything wrong to this woman or her daughter. I always tried to do my best and asked her if I should help her with something, but she always said no to me and got even angry when I did something with her daughter.

I told my mother this, and she simply said, "I am coming to get you. I am searching a flight now and hope I will come tonight, so be ready." We hung up. I lay back in the bed, cried, and thought about everything. I knew I didn't do anything wrong to her. When something wasn't right, it was her, not me.

Eventually I had to go out and eat some food. I prayed that I wouldn't see them, and luckily they weren't at home by the time I walked out of my room. I rushed to get something to eat and drink and head back to my room as fast as I could. I started to pack my things, and tears rolled down my face. After some time, I got a message from my mum that she had booked a flight for tonight, but because of some explosion from a volcano, she wasn't sure it was possible that they could fly.

When I read that message, I started praying. "Please, God, let my mum come here. Guide and protect her during this flight, and let her arrive safely to take me back home. I need her very much this time, and I can't do it without her." The day passed very slowly, and I stayed in my room. When I heard the front door opening, I pretended to sleep, but Ingrid didn't even bother to look in my room and say hello. I didn't hear anything from them the entire evening.

As it got late, I knew my mum was at the airport awaiting her flight. I prayed again and again. I begged God to please let it be all right.

"I am coming. I will be there. Be ready," a final text message from my mum said.

I started crying and was so relieved that she was able to come. I thanked God that he had made it possible. I knew he would protect her during this flight because he was God and knew everything that needed to be done.

It started to get darker outside. I wasn't really sure what time my mum would arrived, but I hoped it would be soon. My things were all packed, and I was ready to leave this woman.

I fell asleep a bit but suddenly got a call from my mum, and I looked out the window. She was waiting for me to come down.

I took my bags, and no one was awake to say goodbye to me. I looked around the apartment, opened the door, and locked it. I left the key under the mat and ran down to my mum. When I opened the door, I couldn't hold my tears back and fell into her arms.

"I am here now," she said.

I hugged her tight and went into the car. We drove to our last apartment near the beach.

"We are lucky that the apartment is free for one week, but after that, we need to find another place," my mum said.

I nodded and said that we would find a way. Nothing was impossible. When we reached our old apartment, we sat down on the balcony and thanked God for this.

I looked at my mum and thought, Every mother is a blessing that no one could replace.

CHAPTER 9

TOGETHER

The first night with my mum next to me again, I slept like a baby. I didn't want her to go again and leave me alone here. However, I still had three more weeks here in Portugal, so we had to search for another apartment or room we could afford.

The next morning, my mum drove me to my school, and Carolina waited for me in front of the gate. "You are back!" she shouted happily.

My mum smiled at her and gave me a big hug before I got out of the car.

"You need to tell what the hell happened, please. I am all ears," Carolina said with a smile.

I told her everything that had happened before and what had been going on during these last couple of days. She also knew that lady was crazy somehow, but she still couldn't believe it.

"I am happy that my mum is here now, and I still have three weeks to go," I said, smiling.

"So are you gonna stay in the same old apartment you rented before?" Carolina asked me.

I explained that we had to be out in about a week,

because new tenants were coming. She held my hand and said that she believed we would find a place.

We went to our classroom and had a small test in English. After the test, we went on a small break and had some nice lunch outside the school. Finally I was able to enjoy my time here again, without being afraid to go home.

After school, my mum picked me up and told me that she had spoken to the man who rented us the apartment. He said that there was another free apartment in the same area, though it was on the first floor.

"Then let's go and see it," I said to her. She nodded and texted the man that we wanted to see it.

In the evening, he came with the keys and showed us around the apartment. It was very empty, with not much inside except two beds, a TV, a kitchen, and a small sofa. It looked a bit creepy to me. There was one tiny room with a big bed that filled the whole room. No pictures, just white walls, and no windows in that one room. It terrified me, but we didn't have any other choice. When we walked out, my mum asked him for how long this one would be available, because we still had three weeks more to go.

"It's just for one week, so for the last week, you will need to find something else.

Or maybe try the hotels," the man said.

We nodded and said that he could tell the owner of the apartment that we would rent this place for the second week.

My mum and I were worried, but we trusted in God all the time. We knew he would make it possible for us. He had done a lot already for us, and we had to enjoy the time we had here.

In the late afternoon, we went to the beach and took

a long walk. It was very lovely and warm, and the ocean looked like it was drawn.

"I could stay here forever," I said, smiling to my mum.

"Me too," she replied.

We sat down on the sand and enjoyed the view and the quiet time. When we walked home, we went to the shopping mall again to eat wok noodles. I loved eating them because they were so delicious. After we finished eating, we went for a small walk around the mall and looked at some things. Before we went home, we had a lovely drive through the beachside. We did this every evening before we went to bed. It was lovely to see the sun going down behind the ocean, and to see that the people were living and not just in the house all evening. They lived there, and that was what I loved about Portugal. I enjoyed living here so much that I didn't want to go back home.

When we reached the apartment, I took a small shower and fell into my bed. I set my alarm and slept straight away. I felt safe, loved, and wanted, and I knew nothing could come between me and my mum.

After one week passed, we had to move out of the old apartment and head to the new one downstairs. The owner gave us the key earlier that day and wished us a nice stay.

When I walked into that apartment, my body shook like a shadow had passed through me. I had goosebumps all over my body for several seconds. I shook my body and went into the bedroom to put down my things. The minute I walked in, a little black cat sat inside the room and stared at me. I loved cats, so I tried to pet it, but the cat ran outside.

My mum and I slept in the same room, because I didn't want to sleep in that small, creepy room next to the main bedroom. The first night, we couldn't really sleep because it was very warm in the room, and we had to leave the door wide open to the balcony. I didn't feel comfortable in that apartment, but at least I had my mum next to me, and I knew that she would protect me and nothing bad would come to us.

After a sleepless night, my alarm rang the next morning because I had to get ready for school again. I woke up, took a shower, and dressed nicely in a lovely white dress with summer shoes. I loved wearing dresses at that time because they made me feel beautiful and more like a woman.

When we reached school, I walked inside and met Carolina and the others in the main hall. We went upstairs together and had Portuguese class, one of the most difficult classes I ever took. I tried my best every day, to get better in it. Carolina tried to teach me some more words every day.

After school, we went out for some lunch near the beach. We talked, laughed, and had a very good time.

When I reached home, my mum looked at me and said, "I got a message from Ingrid saying that I need to pay her fifty euros for the telephone bill."

"I called you so often because I didn't feel safe anymore, and I wanted to hear your voice every day," I said.

She said that we needed to pay this because she wanted to cut this woman out of her energy.

A while later, we went to a small bar in front of our place and near the beach. We sat down and had some fresh lemon juice. Suddenly we saw a woman sitting with a lot of bags on her back. My mum said that she believed she was going around and doing a trip through some cities by herself, on foot. After some time, my mum approached her, and they started talking immediately.

"So right now I am here, and I am searching for a place to stay for one night to get some rest, food and a nice shower," the woman said nicely.

My mum looked at me and back to the woman. "We do have one more room in our apartment, we wouldn't mind for you to stay there for one night, if you like." She smiled at her.

"Yes, of course. That is so kind of you. Thank you so much," the woman said.

After our drinks, we showed her our apartment and the room.

"We know it's small, but I hope it's all right for you," my mum said.

"It's perfect, thank you. Is it all right if take a shower?" the woman asked.

My mum nodded and showed her the kitchen and bathroom. My mum and I were happy that we had some company in that creepy apartment, and the woman seemed very nice.

We went out to eat something small in the village next to the beach and then went home. My mum and the woman, whose name was Alexa, talked a lot during the evening.

I tried to get some rest and went straight to the bedroom to listen to some music and text with my friends. I went to my Facebook and saw all the lovely pictures Carolina and Ana had posted of us. A minute later, I saw that I had another message, but this time from Veronica. I was sure both of them had written it. "Hey, loser, why did you block us? Who do you think you are? That you are special? You are just a loser who never has any friends in life."

I didn't want this message to push me down again, so I

deleted it immediately. After that, I closed my Facebook and listened to music. Every time I heard music, my imagination flew everywhere, and I dreamed a lot about love, friends, and being happy.

I also hoped that one day I would meet my dream guy and fall in love deeply. My dream was to have someone who really loved and appreciated me. I wanted to be with someone whom I loved from the bottom of my heart, feeling the butterflies at the beginning. That was what everybody always said to me, so I was waiting for that feeling.

The woman said she had to leave early the next morning, so before we went to bed, we said goodbye to her.

I had a free day, and my mum and I wanted to go into town to Porto. We got ready and went straight towards Porto. Everybody said it was always very busy on the streets, so we should go early to find a parking space near the centre.

Porto was so beautiful, especially the river with the high bridge. We could walk on the bridge, and we took photos and enjoyed the view from up there. After a long day and long drive back, I fell straight into my bed. I wanted to lie in my bed and do nothing at all.

My mum came to bed too, and we slept straight away. It was like the old days, when I was younger and slept in the bed with my mum. Such a safe feeling.

The sun rose, and we had to look for a place to stay for the last week in Portugal. We called everybody, but no one had an apartment free. We had to go to the hotel. We didn't want to go because it was very expensive during the time we were there, but we didn't have any other choice.

In the evening, we went up to the hill where the hotel was. We immediately got a room with breakfast and a view on the river for the next week. I loved the hotel but knew that it was very expensive, and my mum worried a lot about it.

"It will be OK," I said, trying to calm her down. She smiled at me, and we walked down to the beach and sat down for a while, staring at the ocean and the very blue sky.

The last week at my school arrived very quickly. We moved to the hotel and tried to think positively. My last week in school was very emotional because Carolina and Ana especially didn't want me to go. We had gotten really close and enjoyed our time together. The day before I was going home, we went to the beach and had some dinner together one last time. Everybody from my class was there. We laughed, made photos, and enjoyed each other's company. After a long night, we hugged each other tight with some tears. We knew we eventually would see each other again.

"We will miss you very much, Blondie," they said to me as they waved goodbye. I walked up the hill to my hotel room, packed my stuff, and went straight to sleep. The next morning, we ate some nice breakfast and drove to the airport. When we were inside the airport, I turned around and had a last look at the beautiful city. I wasn't very happy that I had to leave, but I had to finish my school. After that, maybe I would come back and stay. Who knew? Anything was possible.

As they called our flight, we went inside the airplane, sat down, and looked out the window. The flight started, and a small tear rolled down my face. My heart felt so heavy and sad, but I knew this wasn't a forever goodbye.

CHAPTER 10

WOUNDS

The moment we landed in our hometown, I wanted to cry because I was scared to be back. I knew that my old classmates hadn't forgotten me and wouldn't stop bullying me, even though they wouldn't be in the same school with me anymore. When we took our bags from the conveyor belt, I could see my dad outside waiting for us. The second he saw us, he waved and smiled. He walked towards us and hugged us tight. After he took our bags and we went to our car, my mum and dad talked along the way. I kept quiet the whole time. I couldn't stop thinking about too many things and what would happen. I already had negative thoughts. After a forty-five-minute drive, we reached home, and I saw my grandparents standing outside, waiting to welcome us back. "I am so happy that you are back," my grandmother said.

We hugged each other, and after a little chat, I wanted to go inside, unpack my stuff, and lie on my bed for awhile. I went into my Facebook account and had two messages from "Anonymous."

"I heard you are back, bitch. Be careful where you are going."

The second message said a similar thing, so I closed my Facebook and threw my phone.

It's already started, I thought. I had just arrived, and someone already knew I was back. But how did they know? And why couldn't they let me be and deal with their own problems?

I knew that they would have the prom in a few days' time now, and then they would be gone from my old school. One of my old classmates, Mike, wrote me that day and asked if I wanted to come to prom. I immediately said I couldn't come, because I didn't want to deal with any of them ever again. He told me that Sophia, one of the girls who suddenly was against me, had to repeat the class as well, but he wasn't sure we would be in the same class.

When I read that, my heart dropped. Why did this have to happen to me again? If she repeated the class with me, I knew that Lucy, Veronica, and Amelia would still come to the school and maybe pick her up.

I took a deep breath and gazed out the window. I prayed to God in that same moment, "Please, God, protect and guide me through this hard time. I know you already did a lot for me, and I am thankful for that. Amen."

One week passed, and they all had their big day. They posted pictures of themselves in nice dresses. I was still in one of the group chats on Facebook, so I saw all of the videos and photos from that evening. They looked happy, and I thought that I was supposed to be there too, but they had ruined it for me. I left the group to avoid seeing any more.

After some small holidays, the next chapter of my life began. I would go back to school and repeat the final class.

I was very nervous because I didn't know who would be in that class and how everybody would act around me.

The first time I stepped into the class, I saw some familiar face, including Sophia. She sat in the back and smiled slightly at me. I took a deep breath and sat down in front, next to Chloe and Amanda. I had known them before, so I was lucky that I was able to sit next to them.

Amanda and I got really close during this period in school. Sometimes during class, Sophia tried to talk to me, but I couldn't let it happen like that again. I worried that she would go behind my back and run to Veronica or Lucy again. She was always disappointed when I turned her down, but what else should I had done? She wasn't really a help either when everybody turned me down and talked shit about me behind my back.

After a while in my new class, Megan from my old class picked up Chloe from my new class. I liked Chloe; she seemed very confident but was sometimes too loud during class. She had a positive energy with her every day. That was what I adored about her.

"What the hell is that loser doing here?" Megan asked Chloe.

Chloe looked at her and said, "What the hell are you talking about? Do you have a problem, to talk about people that way?" She got angry. She walked towards me, took me by the arm, turned me toward, Megan, and said, "She is my friend, so be nice."

Megan nodded and rolled her eyes, but after that I never heard anything from her again when she picked up Chloe after school.

I was so grateful to have Chloe that time, and I tried to thank her as many times as possible.

During the first term in school, I felt more confident in myself again. When I went out for a break, I didn't mind sitting alone somewhere. I didn't care when no one talked to me during the break. My main focus was that I would finish school with good grades. Then I would be free afterwards.

Surprisingly, the more you don't care about other people or what they think about you, the more they come towards you. I never sat alone or walked alone during the breaks because people came to me. They wanted to be with me and talk to me. The less I cared, the more they cared. That was fact. But to get to this point and be myself without trying to please everyone wasn't easy at all. For me, it was a small success every day. I was very proud of myself to be able to grow. And someone said to me once, "Confidence is not, 'They will like me.' Confidence is, 'I'll be fine if they don't.'" Even my confidence in class was better, and I had really good grades in most subjects except maths and physics. However, that teacher couldn't stand me at all.

My religion teacher once asked me and my mum during a parents evening if I was the girl who got bullies. I said yes with a straight face, and she felt very sorry for me. In her lessons, sometimes I had some struggles, but after that talk, she saw me differently and stood by my side. I was one of the best in the religion class and often had the highest grades in tests. It was not because I knew a lot, but because I had experienced a lot and knew who God was.

Almost none of my friends—if I could really call them friends—liked her as a teacher. But you never knew what was going on at home that made her the way she was. I thought one you should always try to be kind to other people, or else one should keep quiet.

Every day I enjoyed coming to school again. I wasn't terrified anymore, and that feeling was great. I was back and grew a little. That feeling made me so happy.

I also started to go to the dance school again three times a week, and I was able to make new friendships and enjoy myself again. I loved dancing so much, and that was always very important to me. When I was sad or angry, music and dance calmed me down.

When I went back to the dance classes, Lila and Louise came straight to me and asked me so many questions about Portugal. I met some new friends: Olivia, Dee, Luna, Natalia, and Rebecca. They were friendly to me and spoke to me straight away on the first day. We had our first hip-hop class together, and I couldn't get enough of it. I loved it! They invited me into a group chat on my phone, and we talked about meeting up and going out for some food.

I was so amazed and happy that I couldn't stop smiling. Finally, after a lot of struggles, I found myself again. However, I was very careful to get close to someone again— like best friends. I still had a big wound from my history, and I wasn't sure I could trust people enough and not get hurt again.

We had to start training for a big performance that was coming before the summer holidays. I was so excited about it because I loved dancing in that school with all my new friends.

I struggled to show myself when we were in a small group to perform, but over time I tried my best to get better. Olivia was an idol for me because she was so amazing in dance. I wished I had her confidence and style. She danced so simply but was very good. I loved watching her dance, and sometimes I tried to be more like her. It wasn't easy because she had been in dance longer than me and was very strong. She also did breakdance and everything because she had been a part of this school from the beginning. Almost everybody who went there was in it from the beginning.

I did my best to fit in, and it paid off. I had one small solo for the show in my hip—hop class. My heart was so happy, and I couldn't stop smiling at my teacher and thanking him every second. He taught me the steps, and I had to do it in front of everyone alone. I was nervous when he put the music on, but after I finished that solo, everybody cheered and clapped. I blushed but was very happy that I had the support of others.

School time was great as well. It seemed like everything had turned out in a positive way for me. I was myself, was happy, and felt like I was wanted again. One day after school, I saw that Lucy picked up Sophia from school. That moment my heart dropped, and I couldn't move. She looked at me and gave her evil smile. I had to pass her because I needed to get my bike, so I didn't have any choice but to walk towards her.

"See who it is. If you think everything seems fine now, don't worry—I still have some ugly pictures of you and can post them and put you down, bitch," Lucy said. I looked at Sophia, and she looked down.

"Can you move? I need to get my bike," I said to her, angry.

"So, what, are you too fat to pass me?" Lucy laughed at me.

Sophia pulled her aside and let me through. I nodded at Sophia, walked to my bike as quickly as possible, and rode home. I wasn't sure why Sophia did that, because she was never there for me during the time everybody bullied me. But in that moment, I was very glad she did that. I knew if I would have stood there longer, Lucy would say something else to make me feel unloved again.

That day, I met up with Amanda at her house. She was a very good friend of mine, and we had a lot of fun when we got together. Usually we tried to work out together to stay healthy. She was obsessed with getting skinnier, and on that day she looked at me and said, "I am so fat. Look at my legs. Terrible."

I looked at her and shook my head. "You are beautiful the way you are," I said, smiling.

She shook her head and grabbed her belly. She told me she hated her body and couldn't stand herself in the mirror. It broke my heart when I heard that from her, because for me she was very beautiful. But in another way I understood her, because even me I had a lot of doubts about my body. Over time, one saw women on social media with perfect, tight tummies and lean legs. I always thought I was so fat. But for me, I didn't really find the energy to do more than dancing that time.

After a while, when Amanda came to school, she got skinnier every time I saw her. The only food she ate during school time was an apple—nothing more. She didn't even drink a lot, just her and the apple. She seemed satisfied, but I was worried about her. As one time when I went to her house, she didn't eat anything when we had lunch together. She often ate some salad but sometimes not even that.

"Is everything all right with you? You seem very skinny, and I am worried about you," I told her.

"I am fine. I feel great now. I lost my extra weight and am happy now," she replied with a smile.

I looked at her but couldn't really smile, because all I could see was bones.

We practiced every week for our dance show, which was set to be in two months. I got better every time with my solo dance. I had a second one but had to dance with two boys next to me. It was something different, but I loved all the dance choreography from my teacher, and I felt very proud that he had chosen me to be one of the main dancers. It felt like home every time I went through the door of my dance school. My heart opened, and I couldn't stop smiling.

A few weeks passed, and everything seemed as normal as usual. Then I got a very strange message from Carolina, my friend from Portugal. "You know, I thought we were friends, but I think we were never really friends. My boyfriend told me just now that you tried to separate us."

I read that message with wet eyes. "I never did anything like that. Why would I do that? Tell me," I replied.

A minute passed before I got the next message. "Because you think you can do everything just because you are blonde and not fat like me," she wrote.

"I didn't do anything, Carolina, and I don't even know why your boyfriend would say such things. I always appreciated our friendship. Never have I thought about anything like that," I replied. But I never got any message back from her.

I was so sad, and I though, What the hell just happened? I couldn't get my mind around it.

At that time, I didn't know something else was coming again. When I went to school the next day, I saw Lucy, Veronica, and Amelia standing at the bus station with Sophia, smoking as always. I walked past them when I came from the garage for my bike.

"Hey, loser," I heard, and suddenly a hand pushed me down.

"Where do you think you are going?" Lucy yelled at me. She tapped her cigarette ash into my hair. Everybody was laughing and standing around me.

I got up and ran as fast as I could to the bathroom, crying so many tears. I couldn't stop. I couldn't breathe and felt like I wanted to explode inside. My body shook, and I tried to clean up my hair with tears in my eyes. When I calmed down and tried to not look like I was crying so much, I went outside and upstairs to my class. I was very late, but I didn't care. I went inside, sat down, and apologized for being late. My teacher looked at me confused but nodded at me and continued with the lesson. Amanda looked at me and asked if everything was all right. With my face turned down, I nodded. I didn't want to speak to anyone about it.

On the small break, I looked at Sophia, and she slightly smiled at me but I just couldn't believe that she didn't do anything. She laughed like all the others. Then in class, she acted like she was my friend.

The bell rang, and we finally were able to go home. I walked very fast to my bike and rushed home. When I reached home, I went upstairs and lay on my bed to look out my window. Why did this keep happening to me? Why couldn't they just leave me alone? Those and so many more thoughts went through my head. I was frustrated and didn't want to be pushed down again.

That same day, I had my hip-hop class. I was happy that I could go to dance every week and let go of all the stress during class. When I arrived, Lila and Louise gave me a big hug. We went straight inside, and in that lesson I forgot everything that had happened to me.

But the minute I went back into my car, all the thoughts were back and stuck inside my head. I didn't know what to do. All the emotions I had before came right back to me. I felt unwanted and unloved. My parents didn't know anything about it—I didn't tell them because they were so happy that everything had gone so well in school. I didn't want them to worry about me.

Some weeks passed, and my mum recognized that I wasn't eating well. "Is everything OK? You are not eating well. Why?" she asked me. "I am just not that hungry today," I replied.

My mum looked very worried, but I promised her that everything was OK with me and lied that she didn't have to worry.

Every day my mum made me a sandwich for school, or sometimes she gave me money to buy something at the bakery nearby. I took an apple like my friend always did and ate just that. For the first few days, it was very hard to just eat an apple, but after some time I got used to it and threw away the other food so my mum wouldn't notice.

When I was home and we had lunch, I always took a little bit of everything, but sometimes I didn't even finish that.

I thought I had everything under control, and I lost

a little bit of weight, but it wasn't such a big deal. I never understood my mum or my grandmother when they told me to eat more. I didn't listen to them because I didn't see any problem. I wasn't too skinny. I thought I was OK, and I really could afford to lose some more fat from my hips. Then I would be perfect.

No one in class said anything about it, so I knew my parents were making a big deal out of nothing. At least I was happy with my weight, and I knew I had it under control.

Every day my mum asked me how I was and how everything was at school. "You can always talk to me," she added.

I knew that, but everything was fine, and I didn't need to tell her anything.

When I went to dance, I was so happy. I always sweated a lot and couldn't get enough of it. When I came home from dance classes, I always took a very cold shower. I read that showering cold could decrease fat, so every time I did sports, I showered cold in the evening or even during the day.

One day my grandmother and mum came to me and said, "Why don't you eat anything?"

"I am eating," I replied.

"No, you don't. Nothing for days and weeks. You always say you have it under control, but we think you don't have anything under control anymore."

I didn't know what to say and ignored them. I went upstairs to my room without any more words. I heard them whispering downstairs about me, but I spaced out and looked at my mirror. I was almost perfect, and I didn't think I was too skinny. There was still a lot of fat on my hips and stomach.

The next few weeks passed, and I could see the worried face of my mum every day.

"I am fine. Don't worry about me," I said to her as I went to my dance class. It was just a few weeks until our big show, and I was very excited about it.

On that day, Jess also came to me and asked how I was. I looked at her confused and said that I was all right. She nodded but looked me up and down.

I walked away and went to my mum into the car. "Is everything OK?" she asked me.

"Jess just asked me how I was and then looked me up and down. Why?" I said. My mum didn't say anything because she knew I didn't want to hear it. We drove home, and I went straight into the cold shower as always. I weighed myself. I had lost a lot of pounds, but I loved it. I fitted in small jeans, and they looked very good on me when I was thinner. I was like all the models on social media or in the magazines—they looked perfect when they were thin.

I was proud of myself to lose some weight, and I couldn't get enough. Sometimes in school, I didn't need to eat anything at all, and that was a very big deal for me. I didn't worry about food at all during that time, and I never understood why my parents and grandparents worried about me. I was happy. Didn't that count for something?

I had to buy a lot of new clothes because the old ones didn't fit me at all. When I sorted them out, I did it with pleasure. I threw them out of my wardrobe and was happy to buy some new ones. They day I went to the shopping mall, I felt beautiful and confident. A lot of people looked at me, and I felt loved. I didn't want to believe that they looked at me because I was too skinny. I wanted to believe they looked at me because I was finally beautiful.

After a few months, Emily came back to my life all of a sudden. One day she wrote me, and out of the blue we had contact with each other again. She was also amazingly thin, so we had something in common. She didn't tell me I was too skinny; she supported me and was there with me.

During some weekends, we dressed with our best dresses and went out; sometimes we met other people, but most of the time it was just us. Then we went to a restaurant and ate.

We loved our time together. We both fitted in the same clothes and so we were able share our wardrobes. The time with her felt so good. She wanted to get thinner like me. We worked out together sometimes, roller-skating for three hours without food. We supported each other, took a lot of pictures of ourselves, and were happy together.

One night when I came home, my mum waited for me and said while almost crying, "Why are you doing this to yourself? You need to get help. I can't do this anymore."

I stared at her. "I am fine. Why are you saying I have a problem? I am happy." She shook her head and didn't say anything more.

I went upstairs and looked in the mirror but couldn't see a thin girl anymore. I saw fat on my hips, belly, and legs. During the night, I started to work out. I felt stressed and needed to calm down. I needed to get rid of that fat— immediately. I hated myself in the mirror.

"Why am I so fat? Let me be thin," I cried out.

I pushed harder at my workout. I pushed myself until I couldn't breathe anymore, but I couldn't stop. My heart pounded so fast, and after awhile I lay on the floor, not moving a muscle.

The next morning, we had our pre-show. We all had to come to the arena and practice our dance on the stage. At least there, I had some space from all this and could focus on myself.

We practiced almost the whole day, and when we finished, we all went to eat something small, but I couldn't get anything down.

"Are you OK? Why you don't want to eat?" Lila asked me.

"My stomach isn't too well today," I replied with a smile. She nodded and continued eating her food. I tried to eat something like a salad but couldn't get much down.

When I came home, I was excited for the next two days because our performance would take place soon, and my parents, grandparents, and brother would be there to cheer me on.

"I can't wait for you to see the show tomorrow and Sunday. You will like it," I said to my mum, smiling. She looked at me with sad eyes but smiled slightly and nodded.

I went upstairs and felt sad. I knew I was hurting my parents, but they didn't understand that nothing was wrong with me. I simply wanted to be thinner. I didn't think that was something wrong. I hated to see my mum like this, and I started to tell myself that it was all my fault.

"Why am I so stupid and such a burden to everyone? I can't make it right for anyone I love. Everything is my fault. I am such a coward, and I'm ugly and useless," I screamed at myself.

The next day came, and it was our big day for the dance

performance. I went early to settle down before the big show. We did our hair and make-up and did some stretching. Lila's mum took a lot of pictures of us because she worked as a photographer. She did lovely pictures. We all were so happy and free that we didn't worry about anything.

The clock stuck 3.00 p.m., and our show began. Everybody, was nervous but excited at the same time.

First I had to do ballet, and Louise and I giggled before we had to go out. On the stage, I saw my parents and my brother sitting in the audience. They smiled at me and cheered me on. I enjoyed dancing on the stage. The next dance I had was my first hip-hop class, where I had to do my solo dance. "You can do this," my teacher cheered me on. We were all on the stage, and the light shone only on me. Everybody looked at me. I took a deep breath and danced like I was on my own. That dance was magical for me, and I enjoyed dancing with my friends and also doing my solo.

We had a fifteen-minute break in between and were able to go out to see our parents. I went outside and met my parents. "You were great," they said, smiling at me. I hugged them and went straight into the dressing room. I drank some water and warmed up.

My friends and I took some silly pictures and videos during the break. I loved it, and that time was something else. It was stressful for everyone because every show needed to be good, despite all this stress, we kept smiling. When the second part started, we had our repertoire dance group, where I had to start the dance with two male dancers. This time I wasn't too nervous because I knew that dance in my sleep; I loved the choreography very much. The music started, and the light was on us three. Then everybody came out from the sides, and we finished the choreography together. That was my last dance from the show, and I couldn't be happier. And tomorrow would be the same again.

When I came home, I ate something really small to try to make my parents happier with me. But after that meal, I went straight to a cold shower.

The next day arrived, and I couldn't stop smiling the whole morning until I was at the show. It was the same routine, and this time it was more relaxed because we knew the plan and the times we had to go out to dance. This time my grandparents sat in the audience and cheered me on. After the show, my friends wanted to go eat in the restaurant. However, I went home with my grandparents because I didn't want to eat much that evening.

When we reached home, my grandparents were very proud of me and gave me a big hug. I went to my parents and told them how it went. They listened carefully to everything I said.

After some time, I took a shower and went to bed. I was so tired and couldn't help but close my eyes. I thanked God for such a great day and fell asleep right away.

We had two weeks to go until the summer holidays. My parents and I wanted to go to Portugal for a few weeks. I loved the idea of going there again and seeing all my friends, or at least the once who still spoke to me. To this day, I hadn't heard anything back from Carolina. I told Ana and Clara about it, and they were very excited. We hoped to see each other sometime during my stay. We booked the hotel and rented a car online. We simply had to pick it up next to the airport.

The last weeks in school were normal. Amanda did eat a bit more, but she was still very skinny. She was even skinnier than me, so I believed I was still normal for my size. I was just one metre, fifty-five centimetres tall, and my weight was about forty-five kilograms. It wasn't that bad, so why all the panic from my parents?

Every time at lunch, I tried to find an excuse to not eat too much. When I took a small bite from bread or anything, I felt about to vomit. I couldn't get it down but knew I had to show my parents that I had it under control. The whole day I didn't need to eat anything, and I felt fine. I drank some water and lay in my bed, doing nothing too much.

The last week arrived, and we were able to see our dance performance in the dance school on TV. In every class, they brought some snacks, and we sat down and watched the whole show. I felt embarrassed when I had my solo dance and everybody cheered me on in class, but also I felt proud because I knew they supported me. We all hugged each other tight when we finished the classes.

"I will see you soon, after the holiday. Have a great break—you all deserve it," Jess said to us, giving every one of us a big kiss on the cheek.

Finally for our last school day, we had a lovely breakfast together in the morning and watched some movies. Amanda, Chloe, and some pupils from our class sat in a small circle together and talked about some stuff that happened during school and the times we had met up on the weekends.

Sophia also sat in the circle, and she was OK with all of them except me. I didn't mind her being there and tried to ignore her as much as possible.

When we all said goodbye to each other, Sophia

approached me while I was walking to my bike. "Hey, I hope you have a great holiday," she said as she smiled at me.

I turned around and said, "Thanks, you too." Then I rode home without looking back at her.

When I reached home, I started to pack my things for our trip to Portugal. I looked at my phone and had a message from Lucy.

I opened the message and asked how the hell did had gotten my number. "Don't think Sophia likes you now. She is just faking it. You are still a fat loser," Lucy wrote to me.

I immediately deleted it and put my phone aside. No, I didn't want to think about it again. I didn't want to let this get to me. I tried so hard, and because I couldn't control it, I started to work out. When I worked out, I felt free. It was just me. I was able to forget that text message for some time. After my hard workout, I had my usual cold shower.

When I came out of the shower, my mum blocked the way. "Why do you always shower cold?" she asked me. I shook my head and tried to pass her, but she held me back. "Why?" she screamed at me.

"Because when I work out, I need a cold shower after to cool down," I told her as I passed her.

I went upstairs and weighed myself. I had been forty-five kilograms, and now I was down to forty. I looked a t myself but still wasn't happy about my stomach. There was still a lot of fat left, I thought. I tried to squeeze my fat and wanted to cut it off. My dream was to be thin enough to not have any fat on my body.

CHAPTER 11

LOST

We started to drive towards the airport for our vacation. I was so excited and couldn't sit still. I had a big, fat smile. The drive was too long, and I already wanted to be in Portugal.

When we arrived at the airport, my brother took the car back home and left us near the gate. "Have a great time," he said to me.

We hugged each other tight and then went inside to check in. When we went through the security and to A30, on the way to the gate, I saw so many nice models in an underwear shop. "Why can't I look like this?" I said to myself as I moved on.

My mum gave me some snacks, but I told her I didn't need any for now. She angrily took them away, and we sat in silence.

My dad looked at me and said, "You need to eat at least something. I can see your bones already."

I looked at myself and shook my head. "No, that's not true," I said.

Finally our flight started to board, and we were able to go inside. I hated the airplane food; it was very disgusting, and I couldn't get anything down. I was fine with water and no food.

After almost three hours and one change, we finally arrived in Portugal. When I came out of the airport, I was able to breathe freely. It felt like home for me the second I stepped outside the airport.

We walked to the station, where we were able to get our car, and drove straight to the same village my mum and I had lived in previously. Luckily we had a room in the nice hotel we had slept in the last week of my first time here, so we already knew where we had to go. That same evening, we went to the supermarket to buy some essentials, and afterwards we drove by the beach.

When we reached the hotel, we went straight to bed. All of us were very tired because it was a long trip, and the weather was warm outside even during the night. It was very different from our hometown, where it usually rained all day.

When the sun rose and the light shone on my face, I felt the warmth and loving energy through my body. I woke up and looked outside the window towards the river. It was so great to be here, and I smiled. I took a quick shower and put my bikini on under my dress because we wanted to have a nice afternoon at the beach. I messaged my friends Ana and Richard from my school in Portugal to see if we could meet someday soon. Richard wrote me back in a few minutes. "Hello there.

Yes, of course we can meet. I have one more ticket for the festival event here in

Porto, with your favourite DJ playing. Do you want to come?" he wrote.

"Yes, of course. Let me know which day, and I will come," I replied.

I told my parents about it, and they were not sure if they wanted to let me go. They had never really met my friends here except the girls. Richard was gay, and he was very friendly and open to everyone. They told me that they would think about it and tell me in the evening if they were OK with me going. I nodded, and we drove to beach after breakfast. We searched for a nice, sunny spot near the ocean and lay down to tan. My dad always got very red, but he enjoyed being on the beach as much as my mum and I did.

When I saw myself in my bikini, I was still very shy to show my body. I couldn't walk on the beach with just my bikini on—I felt too thick to do that. I simply wanted to lie on my towel and to get some tan.

In Portugal, I started to eat small, a lot of fruits and healthy food. When we went to eat after our beach day, we went straight to the shopping mall. I ordered my wok noodles and tried to eat small but couldn't finish it. My parents looked at me, worried, but I assured them that I was all right. After our dinner, we went for some shopping in the mall. I bought a lovely white dress and some shorts. After our shopping, we went back to the hotel and went straight to our room to sleep.

The next morning, my mum told me that I was allowed to go with my friend to the festival on the beach.

"Oh, thank you so much," I said as I hugged her.

"But we need to see him before you go with him and his mum," she said.

I nodded and immediately wrote him a message that

I could go and that he should let me know how we were going to meet up.

He wrote back, "My mum and I will pick you up. It is in two days in the evening and goes until early morning because there are four DJs doing their music. See you in two days."

I told my mother, and we agreed on them coming to our hotel to pick me up. During the day, I wanted to meet Ana at a cafe near the beach. My parents went to the beach and enjoyed themselves. At 2.00 p.m. I met Ana at our favourite café, and she was already there waiting for me.

"Hello, my love. Long time!" she said as she hugged me tight.

"Yes, too long!" I replied.

We sat down and ate some snacks—or at least she ate some snack. I just drank water.

"So how are you? You look so skinny," Ana said.

"I am doing very good, and now that I am here, I am much better," I replied. I didn't say anything about her skinny comment.

We talked about all sorts of stuff and also Carolina. Ana told me that Carolina and her boyfriend had broken up over onemonthago.

"I don't know exactly what happened, but Carolina got very distant from everyone. She really changed in a bad way," Ana said.

I told her about the message I had received from her a few months back, and Ana said that she had heard something like that but knew it wasn't true.

"Her boyfriend wasn't really loyal, you see," Ana said. I looked at her and was very surprised because they always

137

seemed so in love and happy. They always spoke so sweetly with each other, and it seemed like nothing would separate them. After a long talk, Ana had to go back home, and I had to meet my parents at the beach. We hugged each other tight and promised we would meet again before I left.

I went to the beach and enjoyed the wind, sun, and ocean. It was so relaxing. When I found my parents, I took off my dress and lay down to catch some sun. Meanwhile, my dad went for a walk on the beach, and my mum went into the ocean. Because I was very blonde, everybody looked at me many times. Most of the time I enjoyed the attention, but in another way, some old men were very creepy, and I didn't want them look at me. Therefore I always dressed up when I stood up.

After some hours, we went home to take a quick shower. When we finished, we went out to eat again near the beach, but in the next village. I loved the food there but couldn't finish it. When I got some dessert, I wanted to throw up, but I couldn't let my parents know. Sometimes I went to the bathroom a bit longer so that when I came back, they would be already done with their food, and we would have to go back to the hotel. After our dinner, we went for a small walk along the beach. My mum took some amazing pictures of the beach and me. I loved them very much and knew that if I went back home, I wanted to print them out. When I looked around during our walk, I felt at home, like I was meant to be here and I had known this place for a long time. I never wanted to go back to my hometown. This was my home, and I wanted to stay here as long as possible.

The minute we got to the hotel, we put on the TV and watched a bit, but soon we all very tired and fell asleep.

After two days, finally I was able to meet my friend Richard to go to the festival on the beach. I was so excited to go there because I loved the DJ who would make the concert. We didn't know who else would be playing. They always needed an opening act, and then the main act would show. The whole day I couldn't eat or sit still. I wanted to go there already. Richard and I texted all day, and he told me the time he would pick me up.

My parents always said to me that I should be careful and not get separated from him.

"I know, thank you," I said to them.

Finally the evening came, and I waited outside with my mum for Richard to pick me up. After a few minutes, he and his mum arrived. They introduced themselves to my mum and had a chat.

"I will pick them up. When the concert is done and bring her here again," his mum said to us. My mum nodded, gave me a hug, and told me to take care of myself. She added that I should always have my phone with me.

When we took off, I waved at my mum. Richard looked at me and said, "I am so excited! This will be awesome."

I smiled and looked out the window to see where we were going.

Apart from me being nervous, I thought about all the good things that had happened to me these past few months. Not all memories were good, but most of them were.

After an hour, we reached the concert on the beach. "Richard, you need to text me when I should pick you up again," his mum said to us, and she gave us a kiss on our cheeks.

"Let's go!" Richard screamed happily.

There were so many people and food trucks. He recommended that we first get something to drink and then maybe try a Portuguese hot dog. I nodded my head and moved along with him. It looked so beautiful, with the beach nearby, and all the people were happy. When we got our stamp on our hands, we went to get some drinks. I knew that I wasn't allowed to drink any alcohol because it would damage my diet plan, so I stuck with some lemon juice. Richard had a nice drink for himself, and he enjoyed it until the last sip. We still had thirty minutes to go until the show started, so we decided to get something to eat. "Do you want a large hot dog or a small one?" he asked me.

"I want a tiny one, please," I replied. He laughed at me and ordered two small hot dogs for us.

I must say they were very delicious, but I didn't want to eat any more. Even after that hot dog, I felt guilty. I felt fat instantly and wanted to throw up, but I had to hold it back.

Finally it was the time, and we were in the first lines. Everybody screamed and cheered and jumped up and down. Than the music started, and smoke came from the stage, as well as electric lights. There were dancers, and after some music, the DJ came out and stood on his keypad. Everybody got crazy. It was so amazing. We jumped up and down with everybody, raised our hands in the air, and felt free with no worries.

After a few hours, it was already five in the morning. I got a text message from my mum. "When are you coming home? Is everything OK?"

I replied that we were having a great time and were now waiting for his mum to pick us up.

"I hope my mum will reply soon, or we will have to

camp out here," he said, laughing. I laughed with him, and we sat down on the side of the road.

After an hour and a half, finally his mother arrived. "I am so sorry. I felt asleep and didn't hear my phone," she said guiltily. We smiled at her and said that it was all right. When I sat in the car, I felt exhausted. After an hour's drive, we reached my hotel. I said goodbye to them and gave them a big hug.

"See you soon." they said as they drove off.

I went inside the hotel and into my room. The minute I went inside my room, I fell into my bed and didn't wake up again until the next morning, about two hours after I'd arrived the day previously. My mum stood next to my bed and asked me if I wanted some breakfast. I pulled my blanket over my face and shook my head. They went alone for breakfast and for some shopping in the supermarket. At 1.00 p.m., I finally woke up.

"So you finally managed to wake up," my parents noted, smiling.

"That was a very long night," my mum added.

I nodded my head and said, "But it was amazing." I left to take a long shower and dress nicely.

"We want to go to the beach. Do you want to come?" they asked me.

"Yes, of course," I replied. We went to our car and drove to the beach. We sat down and enjoyed the sun. I was so happy that I didn't need to do anything else because I was still very tired, and my body just wanted to rest.

The next days passed quickly, but I loved every single one. After the two-week holiday in the sun, we sadly had to go back home. We packed our stuff and went to put it in the car. After our breakfast, we had to leave. During the drive, I hoped that this ride would never end and we had to stay here. But unfortunately we arrived at the airport. We left the car at the station where we had picked it up and walked to the airport. After that, we checked in and went inside the airport shops. It was just thirty minutes before we were able to board the plane.

I sat in the plane and wanted to cry. I didn't want to leave because it seemed much easier here than in my hometown. Or maybe it was because I was on holiday. But even during the time I went to school here, I had a great time during and after school. I touched the window, and the pilots started up the plane, and off we went. After one transfer and three hours, we reached home.

My brother waited for us at the airport with our car. "There you are," he said as he hugged us all. We drove back home.

"So how was it? I guess there was better weather than here for sure," he said, still smiling.

My mum talked to him the whole drive and told him everything. And yes, the weather was clearly better than here. We arrived home, and it started to rain. How was that possible? I wanted to go back!

I had three more days until school started again. I wanted to relax and hang with some of my friends from school, like Amanda.

When I met up with her, she was happy to see me and hugged me tight. We took a lot of photos on that day and enjoyed the time together. She was still very thin, but I thought that she looked great, and I wanted to be thin like her.

When I reached home, I went to the bathroom to weigh myself. I saw forty-two kilograms on the scale. "Oh, no, two more than two weeks ago," I said to myself. I was so frustrated when I saw that number, and I wanted to take it out of me. I knew that I hadn't done a lot during the holiday, so it was my fault. I needed to start doing more—right now.

I changed into some workout clothes and started to run outside. After my long run, I took a cold shower. I panicked and was scared that I would gain more weight. My body was fat—I saw it all in the mirror, and I hated it. I hated myself for letting this happen.

CHAPTER 12

LOVE

School started again. I wasn't nervous or excited, but I was happy to see everybody. When I went inside the classroom, my heart stopped. Veronica and Lucy stood inside my classroom, talking to Sophia.

"Oh, hello there. You think just because you deleted us on Facebook, we can't get to you and your ugly face?" Veronica said to me.

They were about to leave, but before they did, Lucy looked at me and said, "You know, your legs look very tight together. I think you should do more sports to get rid of the fat." She laughed and went outside. Everybody stared at me except Sophia. She looked down and didn't say anything.

"Don't mind her. She thinks she can do everything and is the most popular girl in the world. But she isn't," Chloe told me as she gave me a big hug. I felt a bit relieved but thought what she had said about my legs was very much true. I sat down quietly and had so many thoughts in my head. Why couldn't she stop? Why did she have to be everywhere I was? And why did she have to put me down to be happy? Too many questions with no answers, and I knew I would never get them. In school, I was very good. I had good grades and didn't mind being alone during the breaks. I was trying to think positive and smile. When school finished, I went home and listened to some music. I didn't want to eat lunch because I was so tired of eating. I wanted to be thin so Lucy couldn't say anything mean to me. Most times I wanted her to be jealous and want to be friends with me. But probably that would never happen, because she was such a bitch and would always find something else she could criticize. She would always show me that I was bad, ugly, and fat.

My mum called me to come eat. I went down, sat on my seat, and stared at the food. I felt forced to eat the food, but my body blocked me from eating. My mum looked at me and forced me to eat something.

I took small bites and said that I couldn't eat more, because my stomach wasn't OK today. She stared at me and then looked down at her food, a small tear rolling down her face.

I thought, I am sorry that I am disappointing you every day. I am sorry that am such a burden to you, and that you have to worry about me every day. I'm sorry that you had to force me to eat, and maybe you thought I didn't like the food. I have made you sad and depressed. I am sorry, Mum. After lunch, I went upstairs and worked out in my room so Mum wouldn't see it. I sweated so much and wanted to take my cold shower. When I finished, I went out and looked inside the mirror.

"Why am I so ugly?" I said. I hated every part of myself. I wanted to be perfect and feel confident.

I remembered that my dad always said I needed to be stronger, but being strong took a lot of sacrifice. For me, it wasn't easy, because I didn't want anybody hurt or blamed.

After three weeks, my weight was down now to forty kilograms again. I was happy, but I couldn't stop. I didn't want to stop. I was scared I would regain those two kilograms again. I couldn't stop.

My mum was very worried about me and my weight, because sometimes I went to her and told her that I had finally lost some weight. She always looked at me and didn't say anything. I knew she wasn't happy, but I wanted to be happy too, and when I lost weight, I was happy.

The weeks passed, and I lost more and more weight. My mum looked at me one day and said, "It can't continue like this. Don't you see what you are doing to yourself? You need to eat!" She practically screamed and was very angry.

I tried to calm her down and make her believe I had it under control, but after a few more weeks, I knew I didn't have anything under control. Because my appetite was gone, I couldn't eat anything. I could go a whole day or many days without food in my stomach.

When my birthday approached, I had a small coffee and tea party with some of my friends. One of my friends was Anna, the cousin from Nicola; she was very friendly the first time I had met her, and we got along very well. I invited her, Nicola, Amanda, and some of my family. It was a very lovely day, and everybody enjoyed the cake—except me.

My mum told me that maybe it would be good for me if we went to Portugal for a week, when we had our autumn holiday after my birthday.

"Oh, yes, that would be great. Can I take a friend along?" I asked her. She nodded and asked me whom I wanted to take along. I told her that I would like Anna. She would also pay her own way.

My mum was happy about it and accepted it. She told me that my grandmother would come too because she hadn't been to Portugal before. That evening, I talked to Anna, and she agreed at once. We booked the flight and the hotel I felt butterflies in my stomach and was so happy that I had something to look forward to.

On my last day at school before our one-week break, we had a relaxing day, sitting in class and making music. Everybody was happy and enjoyed the time. When I went to my bike, Sophia came to my side. "Hey, can I talk to you?" she asked me as she held my shoulder.

I nodded and told her to continue.

"I am very sorry about what happened with Lucy and Veronica. I don't know why they are still doing this to you."

"But you are still with them and supporting them. Otherwise, you would have gone another way and separated yourself from them. I can't trust you in anything you are saying right now," I said, and I rode straight home without looking back at her.

Maybe I was mean to her, but she knew what she was doing, and she also knew how Lucy thought of me and what she had done to me. I couldn't trust her that easily again. And I didn't want her in my life again after she showed me she wouldn't stand by me in that kind of situation.

The holiday day was around the corner. I packed all my nice dresses and some jeans because this time of the year wasn't too warm. It was October and the beginning of autumn. I was so excited. Anna came to us in the evening because our flight was very early in the morning.

We didn't sleep at all and talked about so many things,

including her current relationship. After some time, we eventually set an alarm for the next morning and fell asleep.

The alarm rang, and my eyes opened. Finally it is time, I thought to myself. I got up, washed my face, and dressed. I wore black trousers, my favourite one since I had lost so much weight because I looked so skinny in them. I also put on my favourite sweatshirt.

"Wow, your legs are really skinny," Anna said it, shocked.

I shrugged. "No, I am far from perfect," I replied as I smiled at her.

We went downstairs and had a small breakfast, some cereal with milk. I had just a little bit because especially in the early morning, I couldn't eat anything.

My thoughts were already in Portugal, and I couldn't wait to be there already. My grandma knocked on our door and came inside. "Hello, everyone. Are you ready to go?" she asked us. Everybody nodded, and off we went. My dad brought all our bags inside our car and drove us to the airport.

Anna and I couldn't stop smiling. It was our first trip together, and I knew she would love it.

Finally, after forty-five minutes without traffic, we reached the airport. Everybody took their luggage, said goodbye to my dad, and went inside the airport lounges. My grandma looked at everything inside, and she even wanted to buy some things again, but we told her that she should save her money for Portugal.

"Flight A235, Gate A14, is ready to board," they announced. We rushed to the gate and were able to sit down immediately. "I hope this flight won't have any turbulence," my grandma said.

"It will be all right," my mum told her.

We listened to some music during the flight, and Anna read her book. Time passed, and we arrived at the transit airport to change to the final flight to

Portugal. We had to be quick but made it just in time. The door to the airport was already open, and we simply had to go inside and sit down.

When we were in the air above the clouds, it looked like paradise. It looked as if it was drawn, and I felt love and the presence of God during that flight. I knew he was there to protect us, and he would never let anyone down with his pure love. After two more hours, we finally reached Portugal. I could already see the ocean and beach when we landed. I was stunned and said, "Wow."

We landed and went out right away. Our luggage came quickly, so we didn't have to wait. When I went outside the airport, I was smiling and couldn't believe I was here again. We went to the car rental and then headed straight to the hotel in the village.

"Wow, this looks awesome," Anna said, stunned.

"Yes, and you will love the hotel and the beach, believe me," I replied.

My grandma and mum talked about their plans while we were here. All I could think about was lying on the beach to enjoy the sun, sand, and ocean.

After a long drive, we finally reached the hotel. My mum and I showed my grandma and Anna everything, and they were amazed, from the view to the river and even the hotel itself.

"I hope the breakfast is good here," Anna said, grinning.

I nodded, and we went up to our hotel room. We had

two separate rooms, but they were next to each other. We jumped into our beds and smiled. We couldn't wait to get outside and enjoy life here.

It was late and we were a bit hungry, so we went to the shopping mall my mum and I knew from earlier visits. We went to eat some wok noodles, and my grandma tried some Portuguese food. I looked at the noodles but couldn't eat them. "Why are you not eating, my child?" my grandma said.

"You need to eat something. You haven't been eating since early morning," my mum said. Everybody looked at me, and I felt stress inside my body. I wanted to run away. I felt pressure and took a bite of my noodles to quiet them, but I didn't enjoy it at all. I felt very sad that they forced me and didn't understand me. The rest of dinner, I was very quiet and tried to focus on something else.

After dinner, we went through the shopping mall and found some nice clothes to buy. In the changing room, Anna looked at me and said, "You know, they are just worried about you. I mean, you do look very skinny. And they are just scared that it's getting out of control."

"I have it under control, OK?" I replied as we walked to the cashier.

When we drove home, I saw the sunset. It was so lovely to see how the sun went down and rose in the morning again. The sun has positive energies, and I wanted to look at it forever.

We arrived at our hotel, and Anna and I walked through the hotel for a while and talked. We sat at the bar, ordered some lemon drinks, and talked almost late into the evening about everything. After some time, we got tired and so went back to our room, falling asleep right away.

That night, I slept like a baby and didn't wake up once during the night. When the sun started shining into our room, I woke up. I went to take a quick shower and get ready. We met in front of our rooms and went together to breakfast. The breakfast was delicious, and there was plenty to choose from, with a lot of fresh fruits. I always chose some fruits and water. I wanted to eat something so I didn't get any comments from my mum or grandma. We sat on the balcony and ate, enjoying the fresh air and that lovely breakfast every day. It felt so free and dreamy.

That day, we wanted to enjoy ourselves on the beach. It wasn't too warm, so we went for a long walk along the beach. My mum and I showed my grandma and Anna everything we knew. We also drove to the next village, where a lot of nice, cheap shops were available. They always had my size, because most people in Portugal were not tall.

The whole day, we walked around the beach and the city. We did some sightseeing and ate lunch at a restaurant near the beach. Anna and I took a lot of pictures with my mum and grandma. We loved the time together and enjoyed every second.

After a long day, we went to the hotel and wanted to try out the inside pool. Anna and I changed into our bikinis and went down to the pool. When we went out of our room, it was very loud and crowded. We weren't sure what was going on, so we went straight to the pool. We sat in the chairs for a while and then went into the pool.

When I came out of the water and showered, I looked in the mirror and saw fat everywhere on my body. I wanted to cry and scream. Why couldn't I lose this fat and be skinny? I took a deep breath, wrapped the towel around myself, and waited for Anna.

When we both finished, we went to the room and dressed in our pyjamas. "Tomorrow, one of my friends here wants to meet us. Do you want to come?" I asked Anna.

"Of course. When?"

"In the evening. We will go for a small walk in the village."

She nodded and got into her bed, and we both slept right away.

The next morning, I woke up and took a cold shower. When we went to breakfast, we saw a lot of men staying in the lobby, waiting to go to their rooms. We looked at them confused and asked ourselves who they were and what they were doing.

Meanwhile, some of them looked at us and smiled. Anna smiled lightly and said to me, "Well, well. They will stay here." She smiled.

I shook my head while smiling and ate my breakfast. When we finished, we went to our car and headed to the big supermarket to buy some water and snacks. We walked around and bought so many snacks for a day trip. Mum and I wanted to go to Porto the next day and show them some sightseeing.

After our trip to the supermarket, we went to the beach and had some lunch. I looked at the food and wanted to pass out. I knew I had to eat something to make them happy, but it was very hard for me every time. The minute I took a small bite of my omelette, I wanted to throw it away, but

I smiled and swallowed it. After that, I drank lots of water and didn't want to touch my food again.

When we finished with our lunch, we went for a walk on the beach. At every corner, they had some small equipment to work out. Anna and I tried some and joked around the whole time. After some time, we sat on the lovely sand and watched the waves. It was quiet, and the ocean was massive and calm. I closed my eyes, tried to think positively, took a deep breath, and smiled.

In the evening, we went to our room because we wanted to get ready to meet some of my friends. I wore a sweatshirt and jeans because it wasn't too warm that evening.

When we were ready, Anna came to me and said, "You know, they are footballers, and they are next to our room!" She then screamed in my ear. "You mean the room next to my room, right here?" I asked.

She took me by the hand and went outside my room. The doors to the next room were wide open.

"You see? I need a picture. Can you please ask? You can speak English better than me. Please?" she begged.

"But you are older than me. Why do I have to go in?" I asked, smiling at her. She took me by the arm and said, "Please, just this one time."

I nodded and knocked on the door. "Hello, excuse me, sorry," I said. I was afraid they wouldn't speak any English, so I spoke very slowly. I went inside and saw one guy who stood up and walked towards me.

"Yes, can I help you?" he said, smiling.

There were four guys inside, and he told me that they didn't speak English, just him.

"My friend would like to have a quick picture with you, if you wouldn't mind," I told him.

"Yes, sure," he said, still smiling. He told the others to get up go outside the room to take pictures with us.

We stood in the hallway and took lovely pictures. They were very friendly and open to us.

"I am Joshua. Nice to meet you."

"My name is Delilah, and that's Anna, and that's my mum," I told him.

He looked at my mum, greeted her, and saw her cross necklace. "I love your necklace. Very nice," he said to her.

"Thank you very much. I like yours as well," my mum replied.

Joshua looked at me and continued smiling. "Can we maybe exchange numbers, or our Facebook names?"

I was very surprised and thought for a moment, because I didn't really know him at all. I didn't even want to take the photo. But I responded yes and gave him my number, and soon we found each other on Facebook.

After some talking, we had to go to meet our friends. We said goodbye, went outside, and walked to the place where we wanted to meet my friends.

"Wow, that was amazing. And he gave you his number! How cool is that?" Anna said to me.

I nodded and smiled but didn't really think about it anymore. It was very exciting, but at that time I didn't have any mind for love or closer friendships with boys, especially given I didn't know him at all. I knew if he wrote me, I needed to take it easy and see who he really was.

When we reached the meeting place, my friends were already there, waiting for us. We walked along the river and talked the whole time. After several hours, Anna and I walked back to the hotel.

When we went inside, I saw Joshua and his football mates standing at the dinner salon. He smiled at me and went inside the room.

"He smiled at you," Anna noted as she jumped up and down.

"Calm down," I said, laughing.

We went up to our room and watched some TV. I didn't want to think about Joshua, but I was happy when he wrote me during the evening. He asked me if I would like to go with him to see the village, adding that he could show me and Anna around.

I showed the message to Anna, and she said, "Of course! Tell him yes."

I wrote him that we would like to go with him and that he should let me know the time and place to meet us tomorrow. After that conversation, we went straight to bed.

The next morning, I looked at my phone and saw that I had four unread messages from him. It said where he would meet us and what time. I woke up Anna, and she jumped up and down.

We took a nice shower and got dressed right away. After we finished, we went up to the breakfast salon and saw Joshua and the others just coming back from breakfast. We smiled to each other, and I went straight upstairs. Because we were meeting up in the evening, we still had some time to get ready and have a nice, relaxing day with my grandma and my mum.

After a long, sunny autumn day, Anna and I had to get

ready to meet Joshua at the river. I dressed in my favourite jeans, a sweatshirt, and my leather jacket.

"You need to get more dressed up," Anna said.

"Why? I feel good like this," I replied.

She rolled her eyes and dressed in a nice shirt with some jeans. When we finished, we walked towards the river, and I already could see Joshua standing at the benches, waiting for us.

"Hello there. So great to see you again," he said as looked deeply into my eyes. He gave each of us kisses on the cheek—that was how people say hello in Portugal—and we started to walk along the river.

"I just wanted to know more about you, and also your friend Anna, if you don't mind," he said with a slight smile.

"Of course. I'll start," Anna responded, and she talked about herself, what she was doing back at home, and how she lived her life. "And what about you?" he asked me.

He came closer to me, and I felt goosebumps on my body. It was so intense, and I was lost in his eyes. "Well, I am still going to school, but hopefully I will be finished by next summer. Then I don't really have a plan yet. But I know that I want to come to Portugal and stay here. I love it here."

He smiled at me and was surprised. "So you love Portugal?"

I nodded and smiled at him. He slightly touched my hand, and I wanted to hold it. I am crazy, right? I thought to myself. I didn't know him, but there was some kind of connection.

As we walked along the beach, he talked about himself and explained what he was doing and where he came from.

"So, yes, I am a footballer, and usually I am in Porto,

but I was on loan for this season to the club in this village," he said.

"That's great. I love football," Anna said right away.

"I have like no idea about football. I am more into dance, so if you want to explain football to me, go ahead, but I can't promise I will remember it," I joked. "How long will you stay here?" he asked.

"It's just two more days, and then we need to get back home," I said.

He looked at me sadly but still smiled at me.

After an hour walk, we got tired and needed to get back to the hotel. He brought us up the hills to the hotel and said goodbye to us. "I hope we will keep in contact," he said, and he looked at me with his lovely brown eyes and warm smile. I nodded and smiled back, but I was very shy towards him most of the time. "Well, now I know he is just interested in you," Anna said quietly.

"You don't remember that he said he liked one girl in his club," I said to her. "Yes, but still he wants to stay in contact with you, so it's nothing serious." she countered.

I thought for a moment, but I didn't want to think any further. If it should happen, it will happen, I thought to myself. At that time, I wasn't sure I was ready for love and a relationship.

The next day, he wrote me during the day and said that it was a shame we had just one day. He hoped we would meet again soon. I stared at the message for a while and smiled. While we were driving to the airport, Joshua and I messaged the whole trip. When we reached the airport, I told him I would contact him when I was home again. We went inside the airport to check in and head straight to the lounge.

"How are you feeling? Did he write you again?" Anna asked me.

"Yes, he did write me—the whole time," I replied with a smile.

She rolled her eyes and looked at her phone. I was very confused about why she did that. But at that time, I didn't want to have any negative thoughts.

We started boarding and sat down next to each other quietly. I listened to music the whole flight.

Anna talked to me after a while in a normal way, so I didn't think anything was wrong between us and let it go.

CHAPTER 13

UNEXPECTED

The day we arrived home, I was exhausted and wanted to sleep. I felt very weak during the day and could barely walk by myself. I felt dizzy and light-headed. I drank a lot of water, but I just could get down any heavy food. And I didn't want to.

One afternoon my mum came into my room and sat down next to me. "I am very worried about you. I thought that maybe the trip to Portugal would change the situation, but unfortunately it didn't. I am not sure what else I can do to help you." She was very sad.

I took her hand and said, "We will get through this." I tried smiling at her.

I knew that I was a burden, or at least that was how I felt when I looked at my mum. She was tired and worried every day.

Each day was a new start for me, and I did want to change on some days, but then I immediately regretted it in the evening when I looked in the mirror. Some nights I cried myself to sleep because I knew I didn't have anything under control anymore. I needed to change but didn't know how.

I had lost a lot more weight during the past few weeks,

and especially when I went back to school, I didn't think of food or drink during school time.

I needed help, but not from strangers. Sometimes you need to heal yourself, even when it's hard at the beginning. But I didn't even know how to start.

One day, Joshua wrote me on Facebook and asked about how I was. He said that he missed his time with me, and he really enjoyed that day with me.

That evening, we texted a lot, and I really liked it. It took my head somewhere else, and I didn't think about my problems at all. He made me feel happy and free again. He told me so much about himself and always said that I was very beautiful. When I read his compliments, I smiled every time. It was so nice to hear that I was beautiful to someone.

He told me that he needed to get ready for an event he was going to with some of his friends from football. He said goodbye to me and promised that he would write me during the next few days.

After that night, I had random thoughts about him. What if I met him for a purpose? But those were just thoughts because at that time, I couldn't think of us being girlfriend and boyfriend. He was like a good friend to me, and I didn't know him well at that time. All I knew was that every person who stepped into my life had a meaning, good or bad.

During school, I tried my best to focus on my last year. I was good at school, my grades were good, and I had some friends who would actually stand up for me if anyone said something against me.

Every morning when I went to school, I wasn't scared

or terrified anymore. I was happy to be able to go to school without anyone bullying me.

Some days, Lucy and Veronica picked up Sophia. Those days weren't easy for me because I didn't want to see them, and they still didn't stop bothering me. They were still trying to push me down the stairs. I tried my best to avoid them, but that was how life went. Sometimes I met them randomly, even when I tried to ignore them. I figured it was because life wanted to challenge me and make me stronger, even when I thought it was not possible. One day I figured I would thank God and see that I had gotten stronger because of it.

After a few days passed, Anna wrote me and wanted to meet up. I hadn't seen her since we had landed back home about four weeks ago. When I reached her house, I knocked on the door, and she opened it.

"Hello. Wow, what happened?" I said, surprised.

"Why?" she asked.

"You are looking much thinner than four weeks ago," I noted.

She shook her head and let me inside. I looked her up and down. She had always been very beautiful the way she was—her body, her face, everything. "Why did you lose so much weight?" I asked her.

"I focused on school and tried to eat healthier. That's all. Don't make a big deal out of it," she said.

I nodded. Usually we wanted to make some salad and bread before we watched a movie, but she didn't eat anything, so I didn't either too. Or at least I was trying to eat, but not much. The salad not even half eaten.

We sat down and talked about everything that had

happened in the last few weeks. She told me about her new boyfriend, school, sports, and education. Than after some time, she asked me about Joshua. "Did he write you again? I bet he forgot already."

"Yes, he did write a few days ago, and he wants to text me tonight," I said. She rolled her eyes and turned away from me. After a while, she started to talk about me and said that I looked like skin and bones. She wondered why I always had to make so much drama out of nothing and why I pulled all attention to myself.

I was very shocked when she threw all these hurtful sentences towards me. I thought she was in the same situation as me, but maybe she didn't recognize it at that time. She was very thin too, maybe not as thin as I was, but she was getting there. Did she just want to make me feel bad?

"I am not making drama, and I am trying to get out of it," I said to her.

"Well, then, good luck," she replied.

After that conversation, we watched our movie in silence. The evening and our movie finished, and I said goodbye and went straight home. Why did she say that to me? Why did she need to put me down like that? I asked myself questions the whole way back home. I knew I would never get answers from her, not unless she saw that she was wrong to say these things to me. But people saw what they wanted to see and not that they may hurt someone else. She would never come to me and apologize. I tried to stay in contact with her during this hard time, and I knew she needed someone to relay on too. I knew what she was going through. I tried my best, and I even went to her house and visited her when I could. She got thinner every time I came over.

No one had it under control. Not her and not even me.

I was very happy during the week when I had my dance classes. It always made me feel like I didn't have any other problems, and I was able to focus on myself and my dance. I had so much fun with my new dance friends, who were nice and open to me every time I came there. We were like a family in that dance school. All of my dance friends included me in everything that they wanted to do during the weekend, and even during the weekdays.

One day when we all met up at a restaurant, Lila said something about Lucy. She looked to one girl from our group and said, "You remember Lucy, right? She got accepted to a school in Berlin now, a contemporary dance school."

"Oh, really? I still follow her on Facebook but am not writing with her a lot," the other girl said.

I looked confused, and they told me that she had attended school a few years back. They didn't really like her because she seemed very arrogant towards everybody and thought she was the best in everything. I took a deep breath and nodded. In one way, I was happy that she had left before I was there, but on the other hand, I was scared now to tell anybody about my time when she had bullied me. I knew that I couldn't tell anybody, at least for now, because I wasn't sure how close they are or were. Even when they said they didn't like her, I had heard that a lot before, so I couldn't trust that.

The evening was very nice and relaxing. We talked about lots of stuff, and they asked me about my school and what I wanted to do after I finished. "I am not sure yet. I wanted to do dance, but I will see what comes," I said to them. "Yes, the same here. Just wait and see for now," Olivia said.

We finished our food and went home afterwards. We said goodbye to each other and hugged tightly.

When I reached home, it was already very late, so I went upstairs and logged on my laptop to check my messages. One was from Joshua. I smiled and opened the message right away.

"Hey, how are you? Write me when you can."

I instantly replied to him and told him that I had been out with friends. After a few minutes, he replied, and that night we talked about a lot of things.

"I really like you. I hope you know that," he said in one message.

I sent him a smiley face and said that I liked him too. After some time, I wanted to go to bed and said goodbye to him. "I hope we will write tomorrow," I said before I signed out.

During the night, I rolled from one side to the other. I couldn't fall asleep. What if he and I became a thing one day? He was a football player. Yes, he was just starting now, but how would it work? I was here, and he lived in Portugal. But I knew in my heart that if it was supposed to be, there would be a way for it to happen. After some time, I eventually fell asleep and dreamed of him.

The sun rose, and I had to get ready for my school day. I was very tired, and my eyes didn't want to open. My mum rushed inside and pulled me out of my bed. "Long night again?" she asked me.

I just smiled. I got myself ready, ate some cereal, and

drank some water. When I finished, I rode my bike to school, like every morning. At 7.35, I reached my school and saw Lucy standing at the garage for the bikes again. My heart dropped. I started to shake, and I tried to look for another place to put my bike, but there was none. I walked towards her and already could see her face lighting up with her evil smile.

"Hello there. Why, you look like you saw a ghost. I mean, look at yourself. You look like a skeleton." She smiled at Sophia when she passed me.

I tried to put my bike down as soon as possible and ran upstairs to my classroom. When I reached my classroom, I saw Chloe and Amanda already sitting down. They turned around and waved at me with a smile. In that moment, I was able to breathe again. Thank God I was here now.

During school time, Amanda and I talked about doing some sports together. She also told me that maybe she would come to my place because her mother forbid her to do any sports. Amanda was very thin. I mean, yes, I was thin, but if my weight was forty kilograms, her weight was thirty-five kilograms, and she was taller, about one metre sixty-five centimetres.

"Why did your mum forbid you to do it?" I asked her.

"Because she said that I can't control what I am doing to my body," she replied. I could understand her mum, but I also could understand her. I knew how it felt when you weren't able to do any sports or were forced to eat something you didn't want to eat. It was torture for a person who was so obsessed with her body and weight.

"You know you can always come to me, and we can do

something, but I am not feeling so conformable with it when your mum said you shouldn't do it," I told her.

She smiled and said, "Well, it's my body, and I know I have it under control." After our conversation, the time flew so fast, and Amanda went home with me. When we reached my house, my mum cooked a nice lunch for us. I tried to eat something small, but Amanda barely ate anything.

"Do you not like it?" my mum asked her.

"I like it. I am just not that hungry. Sorry," she replied. When I finished some of my food, we went upstairs and changed into some more conformable clothes. We then went outside for a walk around the block. We walked for a long time because I had to get rid of the calories I had just eaten.

During the walk, we talked about love and relationships. She told me about her relationship with her boyfriend, whose name was Joshua as well. She told me that she was very happy, but sometimes she felt like he wanted to control her. "Sometimes when I go out with you, and we go for a walk or something, I don't write back right away. He calls me like ten times until I pick up," she said. I stared at her and couldn't believe that. I knew she would never do anything to him because she loved him very much. But it seemed like he didn't want her to be with anybody other than him—not even with me.

The sun went slowly down, and we went back to my house. As we arrived home, her mum stood at my house door, talking to my mum. We were pretty sure about what they were speaking, but we wanted to ignore it, and we smiled at them. "Hey there. Let's go home," her mum said to her.

She went upstairs to get her things, said goodbye to me, gave me a big hug, and got into the car.

When I went inside, my mum asked about Joshua out of the blue. "Did he write you again?" she asked.

"Yes, he did, and we will write today again. He is really nice," I replied.

She winked at me and smiled. After a while, I went upstairs into my room and waited for Joshua to come online to chat with him. After several minutes, he wrote back to me. We talked about our day and what we had been doing this week. "You know, you are very special. I can tell, given the way you are. You are not like the other girls I know," Joshua wrote me.

I smiled at the message and replied, "Thank you. You make me blush. You are great too."

"You deserve so much, and a good man," he said after a while.

"Thank you for saying that. It means a lot."

We had this kind of conversation for a few hours, and it felt like we knew each other very well. It seemed like he wanted to be with me but didn't want to ruin our friendship.

I didn't tell anybody except my parents about Joshua. Sometimes I talked to Anna about it, but every time I did, she got weird towards me, so I stopped. I didn't want anybody to know so that wouldn't tell me anything bad. I didn't want to hear that I shouldn't commit or something like that. It was my decision not anybody else's. Every day I wrote to him was brighter. I enjoyed writing with him and appreciated all the things he said to me.

The year was almost over, and Amanda and I wanted to go out for New Year's Eve, but eventually we stayed at her house. She didn't really want to go out, so we invited her boyfriend and some from our classmates to hang at her house and celebrate with us.

"Three, two, one, happy New Year!" We cheered and clanged our glasses together. We hugged and danced together the whole night. I wrote Joshua a message to wish him a happy new year, and my parents as well. After some time, it was almost morning, and we fell into bed and slept right away.

A new year had started—2012. I knew that this year would bring a lot positives and negatives. There were a few months until we had our final exams. I was nervous because I knew I would have problem in maths. The teacher didn't really like me, so he wanted to give me a bad grade. Even when I did well in that subject, he hated me for no reason.

One afternoon my mum came into my room and asked me the most amazing question. "I thought about having a holiday in Portugal again, in February, when you have a week off. What do you think?" I shouted, "Yes!"

I was so happy when she asked me to go there again. That meant I would be able to see Joshua again, if he had time.

That evening, I wrote Joshua, and he was more excited than me. "I am so happy that you are coming. I can't wait to see you again," he wrote. It was still four weeks to go until the date we would leave for Portugal, but I didn't care. At least I was going!

The four weeks in school and in dance were as normal as possible. I didn't see Lucy or Veronica during that period, but one day I saw Lucy at the school dance. I was so surprised to see her. She spoke to the other girls and said that she wanted to come and say goodbye and thanks. She would do the contemporary class with us.

I looked at her and couldn't move. She came towards me and hugged me. "Hey, I will join you today. I am so happy you are here," she said to me.

I just couldn't say or do anything. I walked into the dressing room in silence and sat down for a while.

"Are you OK?" Lila asked me.

"No, I am not, but it's fine. Don't worry," I replied.

"If you ever want to talk, I am here for you."

I nodded at her and gave her a big hug. Soon after, we went inside the dancing hall and started our warm-up. I wanted to stand in the back, where Lucy wouldn't come. I didn't want to have her here, so why was she here? I thought she had left a long time ago.

During the class, I was shy to do an exercise because I always thought I did it wrong. Every time I looked at Lucy, she laughed, and I blushed and did the step wrong. I couldn't concentrate at all during this class and wanted it to be over. I hid behind Lila and Louise most of the time and wasn't myself. My body couldn't move the way I wanted it to.

Finally after one hour, it was done. I went into the dressing room and ran outside as fast as I could. I was lucky that my mum was already waiting in the car for me. "How was it?" she asked me, smiling.

"Yeah, normal." I didn't want to tell her about Lucy. I knew that this was the last time she would come here—or at least I hoped so.

When we reached home, I went into my room and logged on my laptop. The minute I saw that Joshua wrote me, I was able to smile from my heart and breathe again. We talked the whole evening, and I didn't want it to stop.

I wasn't sure why, because I didn't know him too well, but something between us was real and felt good. I wanted to write with him every day. He made me happy again after a terrible day. Every time we Skyped, my heart skipped a beat when I saw him smiling and singing to me. I didn't know what that feeling was, but I didn't want it to stop. It felt so good.

I could have Skyped with him all night long. He told me even more about himself, and I felt so happy to have met him. We had met in my favourite country, Portugal. I couldn't believe it, but it was destiny that we met and were in the same hotel at the exact same time. I knew that it was meant to be. God had showed us the way and would keep showing us. No one knew what would happen next, but we could trust and try to stay calm.

The next four weeks passed very slowly. I wanted them to be over already so I could go to Portugal. On one weekend, I met Anna on the way home from school.

"Hey, how are you?" I asked her.

"I am great, thanks. And you?"

"I am good too. I will be going to Portugal again for one week," I happily told her. She rolled her eyes and said, "Oh, wow, that's great for you. Have fun."

I didn't say anything else about it again because I sensed that she wasn't happy for me at all. She asked me about Joshua, and I didn't know why, but she always tried to make him look bad. He wasn't bad, and she didn't even know him at all. After some time, I said to her that I needed to head home. We said goodbye, and I drove home without looking back.

Was she jealous? Was she sad I didn't invite her? But she had a boyfriend and told me that she was so happy with him, and she loved spending time with him alone. So what was the problem here?

She was still very slim, slimmer than before I had last seen her, and that was about two weeks ago. I knew I still had the problem too, but I wanted it under control somehow. I couldn't eat a lot, but I tried. It was very hard.

My heart wanted to live and to be able to do things, to still feel pretty and slim without being sick and having a disorder. Yes, saying the word disorder did take a long time. Because I never wanted to admit that I really had that problem. I knew that if I couldn't get it slowly under control, my mum would need to send me to a hospital where they would take care of me. I clearly didn't want that, so I needed to try.

It was very hard because three of my friends also had it, and sometimes they encouraged me to go for jogging with them or not to eat anything during school and after. I was scared because they always said, "If you eat this, it will straight go into your stomach." It made me feel like I wasn't allowed to control anything by myself; they always knew better than me.

Finally the last week passed, and I could pack my bag for my trip to Portugal. I couldn't wait, and I didn't pack too many clothes because I wanted to go shopping in the mall there. I loved the clothes from there, so I thought it would be nice to go shopping with my mum.

The time had come when we needed to say goodbye to

everyone. We hugged everyone tight and drove to the airport with my dad. My dad needed to work and so couldn't come with us this time, but I always loved some girl time with my mum. When we reached the airport, we went to check in as always and said goodbye to my dad before we went inside. I looked around the shops and bought some water, and my mum bought some snakes for the flights. When we went to our area waited for boarding, I wrote Joshua from my telephone.

"I am at the airport now, coming. I can't wait to see you again."

After some minutes, he replied that he couldn't wait either and that he was all ready for me.

I couldn't hold back my smile the whole flight to Portugal. I was happy, exited, and glad that I had the opportunity to come to Portugal again.

After a few hours, we finally were home again. It felt like home to me the second I stepped out of the airport. My heart pounded, and I let the sun shine on me for a while. We went to the rental car shop, got into our car, and drove to the apartment we had had before.

During the ride to our place, I wrote Joshua again and said that we were going to the village now, and I hoped to see him tomorrow. He replied me that he wanted to meet me tomorrow at my apartment. I said of course and told my mum about it right away.

"Then we need to cook something nice tomorrow evening," she said, smiling. I nodded and looked out the window. I didn't think anything but stared at the clouds, sun, and ocean. My mind was all clear, and I felt the warmth inside me from the sun shining on my face. I was satisfied with the situation and everything that was about to happen. I couldn't wait to walk along the beach on a lovely sunny day, just me and thoughts— a nd maybe with Joshua as well.

I thought about my life, how it had turned out. We finally arrived at our apartment. It was very warm in our area, and I couldn't wait to go to the beach. We unpacked our things from the car and met the wife from the man who had rented us the apartment again. My mum and the woman had a lot to talk about; she was also very spiritual and into religion, and her name was Natalia. They enjoyed talking to each other while we unpacked everything. They even exchanged phone numbers and wanted to meet up soon again.

"That was quick, to make a new friend," I said to my mum.

"Well, if you know, you know." That was all she replied to me with a smile. In the evening, we went out for some dinner, but before that we went to the big supermarket that wasn't far from us. We thought about what to cook tomorrow when Joshua would come over because we wanted to make it special for him. He was from Africa, so he didn't know any of our foods. We wanted to do some spaghetti for him. It wasn't something big, but it was something we knew how to make. We bought all the ingredients for the food and a small dessert for later. After our shop and dinner, we drove up and down the beach. I watched the sun set and noted how calm the ocean was.

"This is great," I said.

My mum nodded and smiled, I could see she was in peace and was happy that she was here with me. Worry free—that was what I wanted for her.

The next morning, I got a message from Joshua saying that he would be with us by 6.00 p.m. and couldn't wait to see me again. I felt my heart pounding out of my chest. I couldn't wait to see him and smiled. I also felt butterflies through my stomach. I had originally liked him as a friend, but I wasn't sure anymore. The thoughts and voices in my head were all over, and I couldn't sort them, so I let them come the way they should be. I would go with the flow in life, as someone once said to me, or at least I tried to do that.

Around 5.00 p.m., I dressed nicely for him and put on some fresh make-up. I did my hair and helped my mum with the food. It was just one hour more, and then I would see and hug him again. I felt the adrenaline rise inside my body. I couldn't help but dance throughout this hour, flowing with my body.

Was it love? Was it right? Was it real?

Yes, it was definitely right, but if it was love, I would know now for sure after this week we would spend together. I looked down at my phone and waited for him to say that he was downstairs.

Finally the clock stuck six, and I got a message from him right away. I rushed downstairs and couldn't hold back my smile. He looked so pure and clear to me now.

"Hello, beautiful. Finally we meet again." He came towards me and gave me two kisses on my cheeks. When he kissed my cheeks, I felt the butterflies everywhere. I didn't want him far from me again. "I am so happy you are here again," he said, smiling.

We went upstairs, and my mum welcomed him. We sat down to eat, talk, and enjoy our food. We talked about the weather in our hometown and how it was different from here, how my school went, and many other topics.

After we finished our dinner, I walked with him outside for some time until his driver—yes, he had a driver—picked him up again.

"I want you to come to my place sometime soon, if you would like to," he said. "Of course. Maybe tomorrow, or the next day?" I replied, my heart pounding faster.

He nodded and told me that he would pick me up from my place here, but first he wanted to go with me to the shopping mall in Porto to eat something. After that, we would walk on the beach near his apartment. He told me that he lived with one of his friends he had met here. "He is very friendly, so don't worry."

After our walk, we went back to my place, and his driver was already waiting for him. He gave me a kiss on my cheeks and a tight hug. I loved his smell. He smelled so nice, and I couldn't get enough of it.

He got inside his car and drove off. I went upstairs, and my mum looked at me with a big smile and said, "That was nice, no?" She winked at me.

I nodded and went outside to sit on the balcony for the rest of the nice warm evening.

The next morning, the sun rose, and I woke up from some messages on my phone. Joshua wrote me and told me the time he would come pick me up from my place and where we would go. "Dress nicely like always," he said in the last message.

I replied that I couldn't wait for it and would be ready. I took a quick shower and wanted to go to the beach with my mum.

"It is so beautiful here, like everything is drawn," she said to me as she closed her eyes to breathe in the fresh her.

I could feel that she was happy again, worry free and with nothing on her mind.

We ate some small snacks at the bar on the beach and enjoyed each other's company. I actually started to eat something small again because I felt happy and loved once again.

After some time on the beach, we went to the small village nearby. As we walked through the streets, I saw one shop with small Chinese rings.

"That one looks nice. I could give it to Joshua as a friendship ring," I said to my mum with a happy face.

She smiled at me and said, "Why not? Do it."

I bought the rings, one for him and one for me. I thought that he would like it, and we would always be connected with it. But I told my mum a hundred times that it was a friendship ring, nothing more. Or at least, at first I thought so. I was sure we were just friends, although I had butterflies in my stomach every time I met him. I loved the ring and was very happy that I had bought it. I wasn't sure how he would react, but I wanted to show him that I cared about him very much.

In the late afternoon, he was waiting for me outside with his driver. I wore nice, tight trousers and a lovely flower shirt with some high heels. He stepped out of the car the minute he saw me, gave me a kiss on my cheeks, and held the door open for me.

I sat inside and couldn't stop smiling. When he sat down next to me—very close —he took my hand and said with a smile that he was so happy to be able to spend time with me.

"I have a bit of change of our plans. I hope that's OK with you. We will meet some of my friends—two of them. We will get something to eat with them, and afterwards maybe we could go to the cinema just the two of us, if you like. Then tomorrow we could go to my place."

I nodded and said that it was OK with me. I was quiet the whole ride; he tried to talk to me about anything, but I was very shy.

When we arrived, we walked inside the shopping mall, and he took my hand. My body felt so intense, and I felt my heartbeat going faster every time I looked at him. Why did he take my hand? Why did I have butterflies in my stomach? And how did he look so good to me?

I loved being around him very much. When we met his friends, they greeted me with a welcoming hug. They spoke Portuguese and some African language to each other most of the time. I didn't mind, and Joshua held my hand the whole way to the restaurant. I felt so proud to be here with him and his friends. That he had already introduced me to his friends was a big pleasure, and it felt real.

After we finished eating, Joshua and I went to the cinema together and said goodbye to his friends. We chose an action and romance movie. As we sat down and watched the trailers, I felt his breath near me and his warm body coming closer to me. I looked at him, he looked at me, and we smiled at each other. When

I turned back, the movie was starting. It was getting darker in the room, and he came closer to me. I felt adrenaline going through my body, and the butterflies were still in my stomach.

He looked at me, turned my face towards his, and kissed

me. My body fell for him, and I was so into him during this kiss that I didn't want it to stop. I could feel his heartbeat pounding faster every second when I touched his chest. After some seconds, his lips separated from mine, and we looked at each other deeply. I couldn't do anything but smile at him. Eventually we started to watch the movie, but it was already in the middle. He took me in his arms and rested my head on his shoulder.

The movie finished, and he called his driver to come get us. We waited for him outside and held each other's hand. While we waited, he looked deep into my eyes. I felt the butterflies in my stomach very strong, and they didn't stop.

When the driver arrived, we went inside the car and cuddled the whole way back to my apartment. The minute we arrived, he opened the door for me and took me in his arms. "I hope we will see us tomorrow again, and that maybe you will come to my game on Saturday," he said to me before giving me a kiss on my lips.

He drove off, and I looked after his car and waved. When I went inside, my mum looked at me and started smiling. "So tell me, how was it?" she asked. "It was amazing! He kissed me!" I told her excitely.

My mum kept smiling. I could see that she was very happy for me. I was happy too—very much.

"Did you give him the ring?" she asked me.

"No, I forgot it here, but tomorrow I will give it to him when I go to his place," I replied as I danced around.

During the evening and late into the night, my thoughts were all over. I thought about him and what had just happened. He really had kissed me! I had never expected that from him, but I loved it, and I loved that he took the first step. I wasn't sure about anything, but things got clearer every minute I thought about him. He made me feel so crazy but special. No one ever had made me feel that way. I loved to be around him, and I loved how my body reacted to him. During the time I spent with him, I forgot everything that was around me and what had happened in the past. It was just me and him.

The next day, I received an early message from him. "Good morning, beautiful. How are you? I will pick you up today late in the afternoon, and then we will go to my place. Afterwards, we could go to the beach if you want."

I thought I was dreaming. I was so happy and felt so loved and wanted. I felt cared for given the way he wrote to me, and I loved reading it.

I told my mum about the plans, and she nodded her head and said that it was fine with her, but she wanted to meet him again, to be sure that he was good to me.

I agreed with her and told her that I would speak to him about it. After some time, I took a shower, actually ate a small breakfast, and got myself ready to go to the supermarket with my mum.

Late in the afternoon, we arrived home, and I got myself ready to meet Joshua. I was so excited and couldn't wait. Finally, an hour later he wrote me that he was downstairs waiting for me with the car. I said goodbye to my mum and told her that I would write her when she could pick me up again, because she wanted to see the place too and make sure everything was OK.

I went downstairs and saw him standing as handsome as always in front of his car, waiting for me. He looked up from his phone, smiled at me, came towards me, and gave me a small but deep kiss on my lips. I was lost in his kiss once again. He opened the car door, and I sat inside. Then we drove off to his place. It wasn't far at all, and it was very close to the beach. We parked and went inside his apartment.

"My friend is not here today, so we have some quiet time for ourselves," he told me as he opened the door to his apartment. It was a small but nice place, and I felt very comfortable. He showed me around.

We sat down on the sofa and decided to watch a movie together, but before it started, he told me that he was very into God and that he had saved himself for the right woman. He showed me his Bible that was next to the sofa, and I was stunned that he had read the whole Bible and knew everything written inside. I told him that I believed in God as well, but I had never read the Bible. That said, I was open for anything. In that minute when we talked about it, I remembered that I had the rings in my pocket, so I took them out and felt quiet nervous about giving it to him.

"This is for you. I bought one for you and one for me. I hope you like it," I said to him as I gave him the ring.

He looked at me shocked and gave me a big hug. "Thank you so much. That means a lot to me. Wow, I am in shock," he said to me with a big smile. He put the ring on his finger and starred at it for some time. He looked at me and gave me a deep, loving kiss.

The movie started, and I put my head on his shoulder again and relaxed in his arms. He wrapped them round me, and I didn't want to ever get back out of his arms. I felt so safe and secure with him in that moment.

After a while, my eyes were a bit tired. I closed them a bit, but I wasn't really sleeping. I felt that he looked at me and kissed my forehead. I pretended like I was sleeping, but I felt everything, and I loved that he had arranged this. It seemed like we both really liked each other.

When the movie finished, we walked outside along the beach. It was already dark outside, so we sat down on the sand for a while and stared at the sky, lying next to each other. I could feel his heartbeat getting faster and his breath closer to my lips. He was so warm and loving to me. I didn't want that moment to stop, I wanted to be here with him forever. I turned to him, and we kissed for a long time. Eventually I got a message from my mum saying that she would pick me up now. I wrote her the address, and after some time, she arrived at his apartment. He greeted my mum with a hug and thanked her for letting me stay with him this day. "I wanted to ask if she could sleep at my place tomorrow, if that's OK with you?" She seemed uneasy but eventually said that she was OK with it as long as she knew where I was. We hugged and kissed goodbye, smiled at each other, and waved when I was in the car going home. I couldn't stop smiling, and I still had four more days to be with him until I needed to go back to my hometown and to reality.

The last few days with him were so special. We got closer every day and every second we spent together. We sang to each other, and he sang to me before we fell asleep. I loved being near him and feeling him next to me. It was something special with him that I had never had before.

Sadly, these last few days passed too quickly, and we had to go home. On the last day, I went to his place. We ate together and had a long in walk on the beach.

"I will miss you very much, I hope you know. I really

hope we will see us soon again!" he told me as he looked down at the sand.

"Me too. I really hope so. And maybe you can even come to my place one day," I replied, smiling.

He looked up at me and gave me a big hug and a few lovely kisses. I wanted to cry on his shoulder and didn't want to let him go. It felt so real with him. I didn't want to go back home and leave him here.

When we reached the airport, we parked the car at the rental station and walked to the airport. Along the way, I couldn't really hold back the tears that rolled down my face. I tried to hold it together, but at some point I couldn't anymore. My feelings wanted to come out.

After a long trip back home, I received a message the minute we landed.

"I already miss you so much," Joshua wrote me.

I wanted to cry and wrote back that I missed him too.

When we reached home, we unpacked our stuff and relaxed the rest of the evening. School would start the next day, so I didn't do anything and simply went to my room, listened to music, and talked to Joshua.

The next morning, I went to school as normal and didn't think of anything that could happen. When I put my bike in the garage, I wanted to turn around, but someone held me against the wall.

"Hey, loser. You think you can just ignore and block us? You know that I know everything, and you will never be happy." I instantly knew who that was because I recognized the voice. When I turned around, Lucy pushed me and laughed. Amelia was with her.

After a minute staring at me, they finally walked away. I couldn't stand up and was like glued to the floor.

"Hey, are you OK?" Chloe said as she helped me up.

"Yes, I am fine, thank you," I replied to her, trying to smile.

We walked together to our classroom and sat down. She tried to talk to me about it because she had seen them leave. But I just didn't want to talk about it at all that time. I wanted to forget it.

After school, I wanted to take my bike and ride home, but I couldn't because it was damaged. My tires were flat, and I wouldn't be able to ride it. I had to walk home with my bike. I felt like they were watching me when I walked out of school, but I couldn't see them anywhere. I just wanted to be home already. When I reached home, I told my mum that my bike had been damaged again, so I needed my grandfather to fix it for me.

"What happened?" she asked me.

"Nothing," I replied as I went outside to my grandfather.

I sat down next to him while he was repairing my tires and looked down on the ground. I had really thought everything would be OK now and that I could finally move on, but life didn't want me to. Why did this keep happening to me? Why couldn't I be happy for once? When he was done, I went back to my house and straight to my room. I didn't eat anything because I wasn't hungry at all.

I went to Facebook and saw a message from Joshua. He asked me if we could Skype in the evening. When I read the message, I thanked him for writing and asking for this because it brightened my day.

In the evening, Joshua and I Skyped. After that, we

Skyped every evening together to hear how everything was and what had happened in school and in his football. He was so far from me, and I wanted him to be close to me again. I missed him very much, and every minute it got lonelier without him.

The next few months were all about the final exams. We studied a lot during this time in and out of school. It was very hard, especially because I had to do an oral presentation in maths. I was nervous because I knew the teacher didn't like me at all and would do everything to fail me.

During this period, I didn't really meet up with others very much. My friends and mates from school had school time together, and sometimes we did something small like the cinema or a movie night at home.

We planned all our last day at school and were allowed to make some jokes during school time and at the school hall. There were things like doing actives with the younger ones outside and some water flushes. We were very happy to be able to do that together on our last day.

"I will not miss this school once I am out of it," Chloe said, smiling at me and Amanda.

At this time, I didn't see Lucy or one of the others at my school, but I knew that they would come to our prom night, because Sophia was still friends with them, and they had already told everybody that they would come. At that time, I didn't even want to think about it. I simply wanted to focus on my grades and pass all my final exams.

When I was in Portugal, I bought my prom dress. It was a light pink dress with roses on it. It was something big and special, but I loved that dress and even got the perfect shoes for it: they were pink with roses as well. It was perfect for me. I would be happy to wear this one to my prom night. I hoped in that very moment that Joshua would be able to come and join me and my family. I also wanted Emily, because I liked her with my brother. I knew it wasn't easy, but at least she wanted to come along.

Meanwhile, I had to study hard every day for my exams. I also got worse again with my eating disorder. I didn't want it, but it seemed like I didn't have time to focus on both during this time. I tried my best to eat well, at least on some days. But most of the time I didn't feel like eating anything, because I was so stressed with all the worked we had to do.

After I gained some weight, I lost it again within a few weeks. I could see my parents' faces every day, and it felt like I disappointed them with everything. They were not happy with me, and I thought it was all my fault, as always.

For our music lessons in school, we wanted to sing a song for the final day. We wanted to represent ourselves with a song when we got our certificates. Chloe was our best singer in class, and she sang because she was small and loved doing it. I did the piano, because I had learned it from a teacher who came to our house from time to time. I felt very proud to do it but knew I would be very nervous when the day arrived. But everybody was in this together, so I chose to do it and support my class.

The next few months before our big exams passed by quickly. The final exams came too fast, but I couldn't wait until it was our last day at school. After all the drama I had gone through at this school, I finally felt safe here and at home. I felt like I had found myself all over again. Maybe not all things were fixed, but part of me was happy to be alive and share this moment with my family and friends.

Looking back, my family did everything for me during school and the hard times with bullying. Even though there were some misunderstandings in the beginning and not much support, it changed in a very good way for me afterwards. I appreciated everything my parents did for me. And I thanked God for giving me love, faith, and trust again.

Even when trust was still unsettled, I tried my best to trust again.

I started to fall in love with Joshua. I felt it. Every day we talked to each other, we got closer, and it felt right. It felt good for me, and he was good for me.

I asked Joshua a few weeks before my prom if he would be able to come. I would love to have him here with me and to meet all my family. He replied that he would try to come but would have only two days free. He told me that he really wanted to come, and he would make it possible for me. I was incredibly grateful for him and for everything he had done for me these past few months we had known each other. My life got brighter the day I met him.

After weeks of hard work and learning, we finally had our exams. I was nervous about some subjects but not about others. The first exam we had was German, and I did have a good feeling about it. All the others were fine too, except maths. It was terrible, but I couldn't think straight and couldn't think positively about this exam. I knew I had almost everything wrong, but I couldn't care less about it because I knew all the other exams would be fine. I would do an oral presentation for maths, so I could make it up at that time and be able to show that I could do it even when this teacher wanted me to fail.

After one week, we all got our results, and I was right with my prediction: I had passed all exams except maths. I therefore had to prepare for my presentation. They told me two days prior that there would be one more teacher with the one I knew. I was very happy to hear that because it was the teacher who had stood by me during the hard times I had in this school. I knew I would be able to pass this lesson.

After two more nervous days of studying for maths, I had my presentation. I went inside the classroom, and both of the teachers were sitting at their desks. They gave me a task that I had to fulfill. If I was able to answer it right, I'd pass it. After forty-five minutes, the teacher who hated me stood up, gave me a very low number, and told me that I didn't pass.

"But I did everything right. There are no mistakes," I told him, quite angry.

He couldn't even finish talking, because the other teacher who supported me stood up and said, "Of course you passed. The answer is right, and the way you got to this answer is correct too. Congratulations." She gave me a hug and escorted me out of the classroom without saying anything else.

I stood in front of the classroom and got quiet. After a few minutes, I put a smile on my face and jumped up and down. I had done it! I was able to go home happy. That evening, Joshua wrote me that he would come to my prom. I was so happy and overwhelmed. I couldn't believe that he would really come just for me, to be with me again. He told me that probably he would just make it in time, but he would be there.

I had two more sleepless nights as I thought of the day Joshua would come and see me in my beautiful prom dress.

The next morning, I got ready for our presentation in the morning, where we would get our certificate. We would also sing our song to everyone during the morning ceremony. I was very nervous, and I wore a nice black dress with lovely high heels.

"Are you ready to perform?" our music teacher asked us.

We all nodded our head and went up to the stage, and I went to the piano. I knew I had to start playing the piano so that we could start our performance. The minute I started playing, I focused on my piano and Chloe's singing voice. I was so nervous even during the performance, but I thought that I could do it.

After we finished, everybody cheered us on and stood up. We thanked them for applauding and then walked off the stage to sit down. My parents and my brother were at my school during this ceremony, which was very simple but beautiful. After we finished, I received a message from Joshua that he had landed and would come by taxi to my place.

I couldn't hold back my smile during the end of the ceremony and wanted to get my certificate and get home.

After thirty more minutes, I hugged my friends and then went home to get dressed into my prom clothes. The minute we arrived home, Emily came to my place too, and we both got ready for my prom.

There was a knock on my door. "Hello, it's Joshua."

I opened the door and hugged him tight. I couldn't believe he had really made it. I introduced him to Emily, and we got ready together.

After an hour, we said goodbye to my parents, and the four of us went to the prom. I held Joshua's hand and walked towards the dance salon.

"I need to walk inside with my class, but you will sit with my family in front of the stage, so we will be together afterwards," I told Joshua as I kissed him.

He walked inside with my family and Emily, and I stared at him along the way.

"Who is that? Amanda asked me.

"A good friend of mine I met in Portugal," I replied to her with a smile. She nodded and slightly smiled.

I remembered I had never told her about him because I felt something was a bit weird since my last trip to Portugal. But now she knew, and we were still at the beginning of our relationship. I was happy that he was there, and I didn't want to worry about anything else during this night.

We partnered up and walked inside the prom room. The minute I walked inside, I saw Lucy, Veronica, and Amelia standing at the side, laughing and staring at me. My heart felt heavy, but I wanted to hold it together. I tried to ignore them and walked past them like nothing was wrong.

We did our small partner dance, and after we finished, we were able to sit down with our families.

"That was a nice dance," Emily said, laughing. We took some photos together and laughed a lot during the night.

Amanda came to me with one of her friends and wanted me to introduce her to Joshua. I did so, but immediately afterwards they walked away, and she rolled her eyes at me. I didn't know why, but maybe it was because I hadn't told her about him. Sometimes you need to be careful what you tell people. Not everyone is willing to support you.

After one hour, Joshua and I danced together. When I turned around, I saw Veronica, Lucy, and Amelia standing behind us laughing. They came closer every time Joshua moved to their side, and they giggled so everybody could hear them. Joshua knew about them, and he exactly knew who they were. He didn't even react to their actions, and I was very proud of him.

They made me feel uncomfortable, but I tried to focus on me and Joshua and the fact that I was finally finished with my school.

"Hey, I am sorry to bother you, but I wanted to say I am sorry for everything." Sophia suddenly said to me as she gave me a small hug.

I was in shock and couldn't move. What had just happened? She was the only one who apologized for what had happened.

After that shocking sentence, she walked straight towards the other ones, and they immediately started chatting. Sophia just shook her head the whole time. It seemed she really meant it, but who could know for sure? As long as she was still with them, I couldn't fully trust her, but I appreciated that she had apologized. After a long night, my family, Joshua, and I went home. We all went straight to bed.

"I love being here with you, but you know that I have to leave tomorrow evening again because I have a game on Sunday," Joshua told me as he cuddled me tight like he didn't want to let go.

I rested my head in his arms and lay on his chest. We both felt asleep quickly, and soon the sun rose again. When I opened my eyes, I looked at him and smiled. I felt my heart race and noted the butterflies in my stomach. It felt so good with him, and I wished it could be like this every morning.

We went down to eat some breakfast together with my family. He held my hand, touched my cheek, and kissed me deeply.

"Good morning. Sit down, and let's start eating," my dad said with a big smile on his face, and he showed Joshua where he could sit.

He loved eating the breakfast we had: bread, eggs, and some hot milk. "It is very different from in Africa, but I love it," he told us.

My dad told him that he wanted to barbecue with us before he had to leave.

Joshua didn't know what it was, so my dad wanted to show him.

I never saw my dad so happy with my close friends. Even though my dad's English wasn't perfect, they understood each other somehow, even when they had to use their hands and body language. It was all worth it. Joshua was worth it, I loved the time he was here with me and my family, and I didn't want him to go. After our lovely barbecue together, which he loved, we took some nice photos together in our big garden and then went straight to our car and drove to the airport.

During the ride, we heard some music from his phone. He held my hand and cuddled me the whole ride. I didn't want him to let go of my hand; it felt so good with him.

When we arrived at the airport, we went to the check-in and then to the security line, where we had to say goodbye to each other.

"Goodbye, my love. I will see you soon," he said to me as he gave me a kiss.

I hugged him tight and didn't want to let go. I took a deep breath, looked at him, and gave him one last kiss before he went inside. We waved, and tears ran down my face. I starred after him and tried to breathe regularly. After I went to my car, I immediately received a message from him. "I love you."

My eyes teared up. We had not said it to each other before, but now he did.

I wrote back, "I love you," and had happy tears rolling down my cheeks. Long-distance relationships are not easy. They are built with a lot of trust, faith, and love along the way. I knew we both had something special, so it was worth everything we would go through. We had each other, and God was by our side.

CHAPTER 14

LAST

Joshua showed me how he could sing, and it was lovely. Of course it wasn't all perfect, but he thought he was the best singer at all times, and that was what it made it even funnier. We talked every night. The time was very difficult for us to be separated, but right now I couldn't go to him.

One day I thought about moving to Portugal and being with him, but I wasn't sure what my parents would think about it because I was just seventeen and hadn't even finished my driving license. I had a lot of time because I didn't have school anymore, so I was able to focus on my driving tests. Focusing only on that driving license was difficult because it was a lot to learn, and I was tired of it. However, I knew if my parents would let me go to Portugal to be with Joshua, I needed my driving license beforehand, or else I wouldn't be able to drive anywhere.

A few months later, I met Lucy in a shop. I saw her staring at me with her evil smile, but she was alone—no one else was with her. She walked towards me, smiled at me, and walked past. I was shocked because I was waiting for her to say something mean to me, but she didn't. How was that possible? Or was it because she was alone and so didn't have the confidence to be mean to me? Had she changed? I didn't believe she would really change.

When I walked out of the shop, I took my bike and went home. Lucy stood on one side of the road with Veronica and Amelia, smoking. "Hey, loser, still alive?" Lucy said.

I shook my head and stopped the tears from rolling down my face. I didn't want to let this get to me again.

"How come you have a hot boyfriend? How is it possible he is staying with an ugly duck?" Veronica shouted at me.

I drove off and headed home.

When I reached home, I didn't want to talk to anybody. I went upstairs to my room and to my bed, crying. Why did they still do it? Why couldn't I be happy without them putting me down? Why were they so mean?

All these questions filled my head again. I would never get answers from them, and I was too shy to ask them.

I had to study for my driving license so I could ask my parents to let me move to Portugal. I thought that I needed to focus on the path ahead, not what had happened in the past, but it was hard to think positively. I tried every day to get better.

After more than one month, I took the courage to ask my parents about moving to Portugal. In my hometown, my friends turned away from me all of a sudden, especially Amanda, who was supposed to be a very close friend of mine. She turned away from me, and even when I wrote her, she didn't reply.

I took a deep breath and went downstairs to my parents. "I need to ask you both something," I said, looking down. "I would like to move to Portugal and move in with Joshua."

They looked at me, shocked, and didn't say anything for

a few minutes. Then my mum came towards me and said, "Are you really sure? You would manage alone there? Away from us and home?" She seemed very sad, but I knew that she would understand.

Love takes sacrifices, and I wanted to be with him, because here hadn't felt like home in a very long time. I told them all of that, but they kept quiet.

"We will think about it and tell you later," my dad responded.

I nodded and went upstairs into my room to speak with Joshua. It was always the highlight of my day to talk to him.

The next morning, I looked out my window and stared at the clouds. They had formed so beautifully, and I enjoyed lying and staring at them.

After some time, I got myself ready and went downstairs to eat a small breakfast.

My eating disorder wasn't gone, but it became better each day.

"Good morning," I said to my parents as I sat down.

"We thought about it, and if you really want to, you can go. But one of us will bring you to Portugal and see how everything is going on," my mum told me as she smiled.

I jumped up and hugged both of them tight. "Thank you so much!" I was very happy and couldn't stop smiling.

When I finished my breakfast, I knew I had two more months to go until I could move to him. I needed to pass my driving license tests, and then I would be set to go. I was already nervous and told Joshua right away. He was happy about it when I told him about it, and he couldn't stop smiling as well.

The next few months passed quickly, and the day I

would leave was closer. I told Amanda and some of my old classmates that I would leave my hometown for Portugal. They were surprised and said that it took courage to leave to another country and live without my parents.

Most people were happy for me, but not Amanda. When I wrote her and asked her about meeting up for the last time, she wrote that she didn't need that, and she was fine with me leaving. She didn't believe I would make it alone in a different country.

I was very sad when I read that message from her. I still wasn't sure what had happened between us, but something bothered her a lot. Every time I asked her, she refused the conversation. I kept quiet, but in some moments I couldn't stop thinking about what she didn't want to tell me.

I eventually had to let it go because I wanted to start a new chapter in my life with the love of my life in a new home and in my favourite place. There were a few more days to go, and I became more nervous every day. I hadn't seen him for about five months, and I couldn't wait to jump into his arms again.

The last day in my hometown, I had my driving license test early in the morning. I knew I needed to pass, or else I won't be able to go.

"I hope you are ready for this. It was short notice," My teacher said, clearly nervous. I thought that he might be more nervous than I was.

The man sat down next to me in the car. I started the engine and drove up the road. My feet started to shake, but I needed to control it, or else I would probably make a mistake and fail. I thought about everything good and positive, and that kept me calm during the ride through the town.

When we reached the end, my teacher turned to me and said, "Congratulations, you passed." I was so relived and could see that my teacher could finally breathe again.

We drove home, and I was so happy. Tomorrow I would hold my driving license in my hand with my suitcase, and off I would go.

My parents were very happy for me and surprised me with a nice barcode to buy some new clothes.

"Thank you for everything," I said as I hugged them.

During that evening, I packed my stuff and listened to loud music. I was happy, relieved, and excited to move on with my life with someone who appraised and loved me.

I said goodbye to my dad, grandparents, and brother. I gave them big hugs and kisses. Soon after, I went straight to the airport with my mum next to me.

When we arrived at the airport, I couldn't wait to board the plane. I wrote Joshua and told him that I couldn't wait for us to meet again soon. I smiled the whole flight and couldn't stop. I wanted to cry happy tears. Finally I was able to start a new chapter.

We arrived in Portugal. I stepped out of the airport and saw Joshua waiting for me.

I looked at him and caught his eye. He smiled at me and walked towards me.

"Finally," he said as he hugged me tight and didn't let me go.

My eyes filled with joy. Now I was able to learn how to trust, love, and have faith unconditionally. I had someone who would teach me how to do all this again.

I knew my life would change, but I was ready for it. I was ready to let go of my past as much as I could and move on with my happy life. After such a long time, I felt at home, loved, and secure again.

Although I knew I needed to work on myself. I was ready to move forward..

What you should do if someone gets bullied?

1. If you see people who are being bullied, help them. If you are too scared to approach them and get between the bully and the victims, call or walk towards an adult who can help out.
2. Don't look away. Never walk away and leave the person on the ground. Help others up and give them a hand. Even if they don't appreciate it at that time, still do it. They will thank you later.
3. If you are old enough and confident enough to get between the bully and the victim, do it!
4. Speak up, but in kind words. If you approach the bully, don't scream at them. Let them know you are in control, and scare them away with it.
5. Help the victim in every possible way. Even if you don't know the person well, be kind because you don't know the person's story, and maybe you are the light during the day for them.
6. Don't laugh at victims. Don't cheer the bully on to keep going. If you do that, congratulations—you are a bully too.

List of Advice

If you are in the same situation as Delilah or know someone who is, I want to give you some advice for looking forward, staying positive and believing and having faith in yourself.

1. If you feel like your best friend or even just a classmate is starting to bully you, show them that you don't care about it. Show them that you are the bigger person. I know it is not always easy, because everything is easier said than done, but don't let them control you. You are special, and they are jealous of something about you. That's why they are starting to bully you and push you lower than them. If they see you shine brighter than them, most of your friends can't take it, and they will try to do everything possible to push you down again. Don't let it happen.

2. Don't let them tell you what you should do or say. It is your life, your body, your everything.

3. If you get bullied, don't keep quiet. All people need help sometime in their lives. Your parents, your siblings, and maybe some other friends are there for you. Don't stand alone, because you are not.

4. When you walk into school, and they can't keep their mouths shut and speak about you, hold your head high and walk past them. You are beautiful, wanted, and loved—remember that. You are what they want to be, or else they wouldn't bully you.

5. You probably know that getting bullied is not easy. Everybody knows about it, but too little is done about it. If you stand tall and try to focus more on your needs and not what others think about you, you will break the silence within you. Especially when "friends" are bullying you, it's never easy because you thought you could trust them, but it turns out you can't.

6. If you want to cry, then cry. Let it out, but not in front of them. Go somewhere else and cry. Don't present your weakness to them.

7. Love yourself, respect yourself, and always remember who you are.

8. Make new friends, even when it's hard. Do new things that you never did before. Concentrate on yourself.

9. If someone, especially a teacher, tells you that your friends are not right for you, believe it because people from the outside see things more clearly than you can in that kind of situation.

10. Know that you are loved by your family. Know that everything will turn out all right if you work on yourself. If you do something for yourself and heal the wounds, you will not believe how your life will turn around in a second. Breathe-Remember that those who spend their time looking for the faults in others usually spend no time correcting their own.

11. Butterflies don't know the colour of their wings, but human eyes know how beautiful they are. Likewise, you don't know how good you are, but others can see that you are special, and that's why bullies want to push you down. Never let them do that!

12. You are worth it, and you are irreplaceable. Don't ever forget that!

13. Be you. Work on yourself and love yourself the way you are, and the right people will stay and come to your side.

14. When people are rude to you, they reveal who they are, not who you are. Don't take it personally.

I would like to thank my family, my fiancee and my best friend for always being there for me and supporting me throughout this journey.

A special thank-you to my great Mother, who has always been there for me. She encouraged me to write this Book and share it with people around the World. Thank you for being my Mother. I appreciate everything you do, and I am grateful to be your Daughter.

Thank you all so much.

"You are loved

You are wanted

You have a purpose."